Thanks to the
Liverpool Daily Post & Echo
and Merseyside personalities who
co-operated with this publication.

The Liverpool Connection

by

Ian Hargraves

First published 1992 by Countyvise Limited, 1 & 3 Grove Road, Rock Ferry, Birkenhead, Wirral, Merseyside L42 3XS.

Copyright © Ian Hargraves, 1992.

Photoset and printed by Birkenhead Press Limited, 1 & 3 Grove Road, Rock Ferry, Birkenhead, Merseyside L42 3XS.

ISBN 0 907768 53 9.

Contents

Introduction

Liverpool is an extraordinary place. Not because of its size, its artistic importance or its business activity, but because of its people. No longer the second city of an empire that once spanned the globe, it still exerts a remarkable influence on all who brave its battered and somewhat confusing approaches to live or work there. No matter that once famous buildings like St. George's Hall and the old North Western Railway Hotel lie unused and in danger of dereliction, that the Mersey no longer welcomes a host of great ships, or that thousands have given up all hope of finding employment. A strong, generous heart still beats beneath a crumbling exterior, and a rare, well nigh unique sense of humour lifts even the most hopeless from their temporary despair.

Perhaps more than anything else it is a sense of unity, a feeling of comradeship in the face of indifference from an outside world, that distinguishes the true Liverpudlian from the inhabitants of other big industrial cities. It has shown itself a thousand times, in the generosity of the unemployed as they spare much needed pounds to help the children of Alder Hey Hospital, and in the kindness and understanding of the entire community after the terrible tragedy of Hillsborough. Within the narrowest and humblest streets there is a rare warmth of feeling, a willingness to welcome the newcomer and make him feel at home, that can only be described as inspiring.

Although I had heard stories testifying to this unique togetherness from friends serving in Liverpool Military units like the King's Regiment, I was still somewhat taken aback at the greeting I received when first arriving on Merseyside to join the Daily Post in the early fifties. Venturing into the city aboard a bus, I asked the way to my destination from the conductor, who not only stopped the vehicle specially for my benefit but detailed a couple of willing passengers to act as guides. From that day on, I have felt myself to be an adopted Liverpudlian and benefitted repeatedly from the help and friendship of a thousand inhabitants, many of whose names remain a mystery. I have been critised and occasionally abused by the supporters of Liverpool and Everton football clubs, but always with an underlying goodwill that has taken the sting from the most abrasive remarks. It is, of course, true that the Liverpool sense of humour has a sharp cutting edge but it is none the less therapeutic for that.

A feature of this communal spirit is the way that it endures the passage of both time and distance. In other words, once a Liverpudlian, always a Liverpudlian. Travel to Australia or South

America and you will invariably encounter one or more Scousers, desperately proud of their heritage and only too eager to hear the latest news from Merseyside and exchange reminiscences. Say that you are from London or Manchester or Birmingham, and your hosts may or may not show a polite interest. Say you are from Liverpool, and they will inevitably react in a positive way, if only by asking: "Is it really as terrible as people say?" Like it or hate it, nearly everyone has his own opinion of Liverpool, and is very much aware of both the place and its people.

I say Liverpool, because it has always seemed to me that Merseyside is an artificial label, a name dreamed up by bureaucrats and used only by those who work in the big city, but are rather ashamed of the association. Most of those who live on Merseyside earn their living in Liverpool, directly or indirectly, and should be prepared to admit that fact. Indeed, if all did just that, the city centre would probably be a livelier and more prosperous place than it is at present, at least partly due to the reluctance of people who should know better to return to the city centre at night.

It is, however, the impact Liverpool has on those who live in it or visit it, with which I am mainly concerned. A quite extraordinary number of distinguished people have either grown up in the city and achieved fame extending far beyond its boundaries, or made a reputation for themselves after spending some time there. Politics, the arts, business and sport have all been much enriched by the contribution of Liverpudlians, who have brought a certain flair, imagination and individuality to their chosen professions. Many of them have little in common save a Liverpool background that they are generally only too proud to acknowledge, but they undoubtedly share a rich heritage. And if the world's oceans are no longer dominated by sea captains from Merseyside, there can be few theatres and few concert halls which have not welcomed Liverpool entertainers just as there are few major stadia in Europe which have not, at one time or another, welcomed the Liverpool football team. Britain's first woman judge, Rose Heilbron, came from Liverpool, as did the first British pilot of Concorde, Brian Trubshaw, and I have no doubt that when the first British spaceship eventually arrives on Mars, it will include at least one Liverpool-born astronaut in its crew.

Opposite:
At the heart of a great city. The Liver Buildings, behind one of the famous Mersey Ferries, and who better to be strumming his guitar there than that arch-Liverpudlian Gerry Marsden, the man who made "Ferry 'cross the Mersey" so famous.

tending to bring out the best in people? Even now, I am little wiser, for if most of the people I have chosen have something in common, all differ in many significant ways. Some came from wealthy homes, others from extremely poor ones. Some did well at school, some did not. And if all readily admit their fondness for, and their loyalty to their famous home town, that surely was not of itself a convincing reason for being successful.

A significant reason may be that Liverpool is the kind of place that encourages you to keep your feet firmly on the ground. Even a genuine star earns no special favours on Merseyside, for there have been so many that excellence is expected almost of right. A typical attitude was that shown by one of Everton's best loved footballers, the late W. R. 'Dixie' Dean. When the promising Tommy Lawton seemed to be getting above himself, William Ralph ordered "All the internationals" in the dressing room to stand up. Fourteen did so, to remind the newcomer that here reputations have to be earned on merit over a period of time.

Talk of football comes as a reminder that many outside Merseyside seem to believe the area to be populated exclusively by soccer players, comedians and petty criminals. Needless to say, there are plenty of all three, plus a great many others whose names are well known throughout the world. Liverpool's two Church leaders are both adopted sons of the city, but they have now been here long enough to be identified completely with it, and their magnificent practice of ecumenicalism, has done much to enhance its name wherever Christians meet to practice their faith. Margaret Kelly, the legendary Miss Bluebell, moved from Aigburth to Paris to establish an internationally praised troupe of dancers there, while much more recently Sir Brian Wolfson has moved south to revolutionise the huge Wembley Stadium complex and give England its first world-class sporting venue.

When it comes to identifying famous names in the worlds of sport and entertainment, Liverpool really is spoiled for choice. Famous football managers like Bill Shankly, Harry Catterick, Bob Paisley and Howard Kendall; equally distinguished players like Billy Liddell, Kevin Keegan, Alex Young, Brian Labone, Kenny Dalglish, Bob Latchford and Ian Rush have won international acclaim at both Anfield and Goodison. Boxers like Alan Rudkin, John Conteh and Paul Hodkinson have fought for world titles, martial arts exponents like Ann Hughes, Frank Brennan and Alfie Lewis have all won them. And if John Parrott is the city's first world snooker champion, be sure there are many other talented cuemen in the pipeline.

It was my growing awareness of the many Merseysiders who have gone on to greatness that prompted me to write a book on "The Liverpool Connection", to discover if there might be any common ingredients in their upbringing and experience. Was there something special in the city's atmosphere, a kind of spark ready to ignite the talent of the truly imaginative, or was it a case of a tough challenge

In the world of music, Liverpool is equally prolific. Conductors like Simon Rattle, composers like Richard Stilgoe, jazz giants like George Melly and pop. musicians like the Beatles and the Pacemakers have made Merseyside a Mecca for anyone with a sense of beat or rythmn in their blood. One of the greatest, the late John Lennon, is still revered 20 years after his assasination, another, Paul McCartney is currently planning to establish a school of performing arts in his old home town.

In the past, many have joked that you need to be a comedian to survive on Merseyside, and let us face it, many of the inhabitants do have a natural talent in that direction. Tommy Handley of ITMA fame captivated wartime radio audiences who also chuckled at the performances of Rob Wilton, Ted Ray, Derek Guyler and Arthur Askey. That tradition shows no sign of dying out, for Jimmy Tarbuck, Stan Boardman, Tom O'Connor and best known of all, Ken Dodd, remain well to the fore of the laughter-making profession. The Liverpool stage, which threw up such giants as Rex Harrison and Michael Redgrave still enjoys the talent of Rita Tushingham and Glenda Jackson, while Cilla Black is but one of a modern breed of television entertainers. Wherever one looks, the story is much the same. Writers, impressarios, producers, managers and of course innumerable artistes all bear the Liverpool stamp that may not guarantee automatic success but does hint at a lively and imaginative approach.

Even in business, not an area automatically associated with modern Liverpool achievement, the city's sons (and daughters) have made their mark, usually through originality and enterprise rather than efficiency of production. The Moores brothers founded the vast Littlewoods Pools empire, which later spread to take in mail order and stores, George Davis built up Next from nothing, Alan Paul became the nation's biggest hairdresser. The city which welcomed Britain's first Woolworth store and saw the birth of the Owen Owen family drapery business is still capable of sprouting new enterprises and ideas.

In medicine, law, veterinary surgery and most other professional spheres, Liverpool is similarly influential. It houses the world's first school of tropical medicine, its most dynamic children's hospital and one of the finest multi-racial maternity units to be found anywhere. Its pioneers have reached the four corners of the earth, and if there are no longer the formidable array of privateers, pirates and slavers who once made its sailors feared wherever a sail could be seen, it can point with pride to the fact that it was Liverpool that Falkland hero Simon Weston selected as the centre for his Weston Spirit young people's enterprise.

Many Liverpool people have, of course, been forced by economic neccesity to climb on their bikes and seek their fortune elsewhere; others have found that even today it is still possible to stay in the area and prosper. Those I have selected include some from both categories, as well as two or three who arrived from far afield to make their reputation here. All have been successful in their own way, all are proud to wear the Liverpool label, all have contributed greatly to the quality of life, not only on Merseyside but in the country as a whole.

Indeed, that fact cannot be emphasised too strongly. Although there are doubtless as many selfish folk on Merseyside as in any other big industrial region, the majority are warm-hearted, kind and generous to a fault. Scruffy, disorganised, bloody-minded at times and unwilling to be pushed around, particularly by bureaucrats from London, they may be, but never indifferent to the problems of others. As my Dynamic Dozen demonstrate, no one city has thrown up so many who have influenced the progress of humanity.

Selecting suitable representatives was not an easy task. Once I sat down to sift through the various candidates. I became aware of the problem posed by their very numbers. So many sons and daughters of the city have excelled at music, sport and the arts that it was impossible to make other than a random selection, choosing people who seemed especially symbolic of their chosen profession. Lord Derby, though hardly most people's idea of a Liverpudlian, has long established links that include former command of its most famous regiment; Archbishop Warlock has been a pioneer of Liverpool's ecumenical crusade; Harold Francis is still a world leader in the battle to prevent over-population.

I have tried, so far as possible, to spread the net wide and include people from many different walks of life, to emphasise the width of Liverpool's contribution. If I may adapt Malvolio's letter in Twelfth Night, some were born great, some achieved greatness and some had greatness thrust upon them. So far as I am concerned, they are merely among the best known of the many, many remarkable citizens of Liverpool who have helped to ensure that, for all its sea of troubles, it remains the principal catalyst of human achievement in modern Britain.

Edwina Currie

Although she has never held high office, there are few politicians anywhere who arc better known than Liverpool-born Edwina Currie, the outspoken M.P. for Derbyshire South who has never been afraid to admit that a British egg might have its imperfections. Dark, vivacious and full of energy, she had rarely been out of the headlines even before she was involved in the great salmonella controversy of December 1988, which forced her to resign as Under-Secretary to the Department of Health and Social Security, after stating that most of the nation's egg production was infected with salmonella. Such a gaffe might have destroyed a lesser person, but to her credit, Mrs Currie has bounced back so strongly that she is already being tipped as a future member of the Cabinet.

The lady who grew up in a poor but caring home in South Liverpool has never been afraid to speak her mind. Soon after taking office, she startled businessmen by advising them to take their wives with them on trips abroad so they would not feel the need to 'sleep around' and expose themselves to Aids. Old folk fearing hypothermia in unheated dwellings were advised to wear long johns and woolly hats in winter, and Northerners in general were told to watch their diet, and get their weight down by eating fewer fish and chips.

Such comments were hardly popular or diplomatic, even when as in many cases, they made good sense. But Edwina has ever been one for plain speaking since her earliest days at school. "One of my first and most abiding memories is of my headmistress at Mosspits Lane Primary School in Wavertree", she recalls. "She was a lovely lady, called Miss Lyons, and she set us all a marvellous example. She may have been rather small in stature, but to us she was a giant, and the things she taught us have stayed with me to this day. She was always immaculately turned out, remarkably so for a teacher, with a smart suit, high heeled shoes and her hair piled on the top of her head. It wasn't so much that she was a great academic. It was the things she emphasised about behaviour and attitude and responsibility and honesty that left such a lasting impression. Every Friday she used to tell us stories in assembly with a moral in them, like that of Titus Oates walking out into the snow to try and save his companions.

"I can still see her waggling her finger at us as she insisted 'You must always do your best'. She was particular about good manners and politeness, qualities that are not nearly as common now as they were in her day. A great deal has been said about trying to improve

A smart and stylish lady. Edwina Currie knows the value of making a good impression.

educational standards in our schools, but personally I believe we need more teachers like Miss Lyons, who taught her pupils to set high standards for themselves and refuse to accept second best".

From Mosspits Lane, Mrs Currie went on to Liverpool Institute For Girls, whence she won a scholarship to Oxford University. "I still had no idea what I wanted to do", she admits. "Opportunities for girls were very limited in the sixties. They could be teachers or nurses or secretaries, and that was it. There wasn't a great deal of choice. I was vaguely interested in politics, but it wasn't a consuming passion at that time. I remember joining the Liverpool Parliamentary Debating Society, who met regularly in the Municipal Annexe, and taking part in their debates just for fun. It had been established for more than 100 years — I don't know what has happened to it now —

and I achieved the position there of Minister for Education. Edward Boyle was the actual Minister at the time, and I think he came down for one of the debates, though it hasn't left much of impression".

Mrs Currie gained her scholarship in the autumn, and typically refused to waste the intervening period before the next student year. "I decided to go to the United States, where I had an auntie who could put me up", she says. "We hadn't any money, so I got myself a job in Dista Products in Speke to raise the fare. It was a horrible place, sloppy and smelly, but the money was good so I stuck it out for three months. It was my first experience of manufacturing and of Liverpool industry, and I made up my mind then and there: 'Never again'. Dista made pharmaceutical products and there was a nasty smell in the air that stuck to your clothes and stayed with you when you went home.

"However, that wasn't the worst part of it, which was the total lack of pride. The company had just been taken over by an American giant, Eli Lilly, who sent a team down to look round their new factory. It was like a Royal inspection of an army barracks, everything had to be cleaned and polished or whitewashed, and flowers appeared miraculously the day before they arrived. The moment the visit was over, everything went back to normal, and the flowers disappeared. It was then I made up my mind that I wouldn't be coming back to Liverpool. There had to be something better".

Once in the United States, Mrs Currie wasted no time getting down to work again, this time as a comptometer operator. "It was all rather boring, because I spent most of the day just adding up rows of figures, but it did give me the chance to see something of America and learn a little about their way of life", she points out. "In fact, it was while I was in the United States that I made up my mind that I wanted to become seriously involved in politics. I was disturbed by the fact that so few people there had any political knowledge at all, and had no idea what their own Government were doing. It was in the middle of the Vietnam war, and people seemed totally confused as to why their husbands and sons were getting killed out there".

Back in England, Mrs Currie started a degree course at St. Anne's College, Oxford, but switched to economic and social history after six weeks. "I seemed to spend a lot of my time arguing with my tutors", she admits, "but I suppose that is not unusual for a student. I was also active at the Oxford Union, though I never quite made President. I did manage to become both Treasurer and Librarian at different times, and felt quite pleased with myself because that was exactly what Harold McMillan, who had always been my great hero, had achieved. I became more and more interested in politics without finding a major cause. Harold Wilson was Prime Minister, so there seemed to be a lot of wheeling and dealing going on all the time, and I could not discover any clear cut Tory philosophy either. So far as I was concerned, that only emerged quite a long time later".

Although her mother wanted her to become a hairdresser ("She still does, in her heart of hearts", says Edwina) Mrs Currie was now determined to embrace a political career. To do that successfully she needed an income, and accordingly decided to join a firm of chartered accountants in London. "Nothing went at all as I intended", she discloses. "I joined this excellent firm. Arthur Anderson, and almost immediately met my future husband, Ray. We got on brilliantly from the start, but the problem was that the firm disapproved strongly of internal fraternisation. And we fraternised very closely! Something had to be done, and we decided that Ray, who was much further advanced in his career, would stay on with Arthur Anderson, while I looked for another job. The long term plan was that he would earn the money, and I would concentrate on politics".

The next few years were the most hectic in Mrs Currie's life, and gave her a vivid insight into the problems encountered by many working mothers. After a few months with the Civil Service ("I've never been so bored in my life") and a year's course studying economic history at the London School of Economics, she got married, moved to a small house in West London complete with puppy and embarked on a teaching career. "I taught at school, at college, at adult literacy classes and at the Open University", she says. "And I loved it. Nothing is more rewarding than teaching, and nothing represents a greater challenge. It forces you to practice self-discipline, and to approach problems in a logical way".

All the time, her work was directing her towards a political career. "Teaching and politics are closely connected", she explains. "You have to communicate properly in both fields, leading people forward from a position they already understand. That way they can accept and remember the message you are trying to drive home. I grew accustomed to setting out my arguments so they could be readily understood, and that applied just as much to making speeches as writing essays or articles".

The next turning point in Edwina Currie's life was the transfer from London to the Midlands, which saw her move into practical politics via Birmingham City Council. "I never really liked London", she admits. "I found a certain lack of identity there. Ray didn't like it either, having been born in Yorkshire and brought up in Devon, so he asked his firm for a move. They sent us to Birmingham, and it was the best thing that ever happened to us. I know the area does not always seem all that attractive at first sight, but the Midlands does have a tradition of hard work and commitment to the job, plus consideration for other people.

"We moved into a house on the Cadbury Estate, and found the old Quaker philosphy still pervaded everything. There were no pubs and believe it or not, before we could move into the house we had just bought, we had to sign a pledge that we would not brew alcohol there! On the other hand, everything was in beautiful condition, litter was virtually unheard-of, and there were at least two fruit trees in every garden.

"I suppose it was a sort of benevolent dictatorship, but it seemed to work remarkably well. We found our neighbours friendly, modest and kind, though they were not too keen on the wisecracks that come naturally to someone raised in Liverpool. We were made to feel at home very quickly, and it may have helped that we were bringing up a young family. As I have said before, it was a hectic time, because I also had a job and soon after we arrived I was elected to Birmingham City Council, on which I served for 11 years. At various times I was chairman of both the Social Services and Housing Committees and I also served on the Community Relations Council. It was great fun and I like to think a good deal was achieved".

Still a Liverpudlian at heart ("Once a Scouser, you're always a Scouser") Mrs Currie believes her experiences in Birmingham, and more recently in Derbyshire have valuable lessons for Liverpool. "I know Merseyside has suffered terrible problems, some of which date back to before the war", she agrees. "But there has to be a way forward. You could see the decline setting in when I was at school. The city was much bigger then, but the writing was on the wall. Even in 1954 the Japanese had overtaken Britain in shipping tonnage and it was clear there was little idea how to cope, because our merchants and shipowners had become so accustomed to a protected market. They just did not know how to compete.

"I know that when Harold Wilson was Prime Minister he made a great effort to provide jobs in place of those being lost through the contraction of the port, and encouraged major industries like Ford and Vauxhall to move to Merseyside. That seemed an excellent thing to do at the time, but in hindsight I wonder if the area was really moving in the right direction. Merseyside had always been dominated by service industries, like shipping and trading, and had no history of disciplined, routine work to a strict timetable, which is so essential to success in manufacturing. Almost inevitably that lack of experience and background led to industrial relation problems

11

The family must always come first. Mrs. Currie steps out with her two sons.

that have given the area a bad name. I wonder whether it would have been better for Liverpool and its dependent areas to have tried to concentrate on its undoubted strengths. Personally I think it might have been better to place the emphasis on humour and entertainment, where we have always led the way.

There is a tremendous boom in tourism these days, and the Liverpool area is splendidly endowed with places for people to visit. The city leads the world in pop music, it has its own philharmonic orchestra, its own art galleries including the Tate, two highly successful football teams and any number of outstanding buildings. It also has the river, and there are plenty of cities in the United Kingdom who would love to have a major waterway in their midst. Don't forget that 100 years ago, Liverpool was known as a city of culture that put Manchester completely in the shade.

"What it must do, if it is to make the most of these immense assets, is clean up and generally improve the environment. You cannot expect people to visit a city if there is litter knee-deep in the streets, broken windows everywhere, graffiti on the walls, and the threat of violence in the city centre at night. I don't live there, but my mother does, and I go back there with my children from time to time to look up old friends. In fact my daughter's favourite outing is across the Mersey by ferry to visit Beattie's store in Birkenhead. There seems to be a general feeling of depression and apathy, and that has to be got rid of if Liverpool is to thrive again".

Mrs Currie puts the responsibility for much needed change fairly and squarely on the shoulders of Liverpool City Council. "They are responsible for the environment, and it is up to them to put matters right", she says emphatically. "That means a drastic change in priorities. From what I have heard and seen, they spend far too much time playing politics. Elected representatives should not be trying to run departments themselves. They should concentrate on basic policy and then keep an eye on the officers to make sure that policy is properly carried out.

"When I was on the Council in Birmingham we decided to have a full scale blitz on the condition of the place. We had people out every day scouring the streets for signs of vandalism and graffiti and the moment it was found, we moved to put it right. Our target was to try and make sure that every bit of graffiti scrawled on a wall during the night was removed by morning, and every single window replaced. And I do mean replaced, not just boarded up. I know that can mean using a lot of manpower but it is well worth it. Look at Disneyland and Alton Towers. One of the reasons they are so successful is that everyone who works there goes round picking up litter whenever he

13

has a spare moment. I believe much the same happened during Liverpool's Garden Festival, and it can make a fantastic difference to a place's appearance.

"There is nothing that encourages mindless vandalism so much as the sight of a street or building lying empty or in an obvious state of neglect. We found from personal experience, that if a young idiot put a stone through a window in the evening and then found nothing to show for it the next day, he gave up in disgust and left the place alone. I know all that costs money, but believe me, it costs a lot less than having to renovate buildings that have been virtually wrecked. And if you concentrate on improving the environment in this way, you can usually count on the support of the residents, who don't want to live in a dump any more than you.

"Security is even more important. Unless people know they can walk about safely in the city centre at night, and park their cars without having them stolen or damaged, they will simply stay away. If you want to encourage theatres and concert halls and night life and good restaurants, you must create a situation where it is safe and easy for people to visit them. That means providing safe parking (preferably cheaply too) and well lit streets where people can see what is happening.

"The vital thing for everyone to realise is that in the last resort, it's up to them. It is no use at all expecting someone else from outside to come in and put everything right, because they won't. Liverpudlians must surely have seen what happens when professional planners come in and suggest schemes without consulting local people, and they should know that the only way to create the kind of city they want is for them to get involved themselves. Unfortunately, Liverpudlians seem to have lost some of their natural independence in recent years, which is a great pity. If you look at the things that they **do** do themselves, like music and football, they are brilliantly successful, so it is only reasonable to suppose that if they showed the same interest and common sense in running the city, there would be a considerable improvement.

"To be honest, I don't know how some councillors manage to spend so much time at meetings and attending conferences. I know when I was on Birmingham City Council, I was kept so busy I only got to the party conference twice. Liverpool needs to develop a feeling for partnership, involving all sections of the community, from businessmen to the unemployed, in much the same way that Glasgow has done. There is an amazing amount of individual talent in Liverpool, as we are constantly reminded. It just needs to be harnessed and pointed in the right direction".

One of the key factors in this partnership approach has to be recognition of the fact that no city can prosper without a healthy business community, and no business community can survive unless it is able to make a reasonable profit. Mrs Currie believes passionately in the value of personal and private initiative, and says Liverpool must come to terms with the reality of living in a competitive world. "There are too many people there at the moment who are only interested in persuading other people to put money in their pockets for the minimum of effort", she claims. "Wouldn't it be marvellous if the City were to say 'Stop!' We are not taking any more handouts from anyone, and we are going to sort out our problems ourselves?

"Shops and businesses will not come to Liverpool unless they believe they can prosper there, and they will not do that if they are faced with prohibitive rates and given very little in return.

"One of the attractive things about Derbyshire, where I now live, is the pride that flourishes throughout the county. Derbyshire has had its problems just like Merseyside, look at the effect of all the pit closures as an example, but it has never had a penny in grant aid. They just get down to the business in hand and work out their own salvation.

"Not long ago we were battling with several other locations to try and persuade Toyota to build a new plant near Derby. There was always the temptation to tell the Japanese how much we needed them, how many jobs their factory would bring, and what an effect their presence would have on the area. Thankfully, we didn't. We concentrated on emphasising what we could do for **them** which was what they wanted to hear. We showed them how good the communications were, told them we had a skilled labour force waiting on the doorstep, and emphasised what a nice place it was for their people to live. We got the factory.

"At one time I was worried that our people would not be too keen to work for a Japanese company, but I couldn't have been more wrong. One senior union official told me: 'The Japanese are fine. The bosses are in before we are, they stay later than we do, they wear the same dress in the factory, use the same car park and canteen, and are willing to listen to everyone's ideas. That's what many of us thought would happen with nationalisation, but it didn't".

Mrs Currie believes private enterprise could have done much more to ease Liverpool's housing problems, had it been given the chance. "The city appears to have been obsessed with building new houses itself, instead of devoting more effort to renovation and bringing in

outside firms to build private estates", she says. "Housing has gobbled up far too much of its resources unnecessarily. The place seems to be full of empty buildings waiting for repair, and several post-war blocks have had to be pulled down. When I was chairman of the housing committee in Birmingham, I brought in Wimpey's to build whole estates, and the system worked well.

"I know Liverpool started a similar scheme with Barrett's in Myrtle Street, but it didn't work because the city reneged on the deal. The problem seems to be the failure to recognise that there is nothing wrong with making a profit, so long as you deliver the goods on time. Profit is not a dirty word. You don't have to be a business expert or a top academic to know that people will always work better and faster if they know there is something in it for them".

One of comparatively few women Members of Parliament, Mrs Currie believes that women should play a much more important role in society, though she is nothing like the popular image of a militant women's Libber. Well dressed, attractive, and extremely feminine, she agrees that women have a vital role in the home, as wives and mothers, but believes they should also look much further afield for fulfilment. "On the face of it we are a matriarchy, with a Queen and, until recently, a woman Prime Minister", she points out. "In fact, women do not wield nearly enough influence, usually because they are too ready to be side-tracked. In recent years, society has come to appreciate that women can do a great many jobs that used to be regarded as the prerogative of men, and what's more, do them very well. What women want, in my opinion, is the opportunity to work, whatever their circumstances, and to be appreciated in the workplace. Women can be very good at marketing and management and politics, given the proper opportunity. of course they have to seize that opportunity when it comes their way, and I think I can say that I did".

Because of her high profile and penchant for making quotable remarks, Edwina Currie has suffered more than most from the tabloid National Press. "At the time of the salmonella affair, I had to go into hiding with my family for three or four days", she recalls. "It was like something out of 'Thirty Nine Steps'. We sneaked off to a friend's house, while an army of 30-40 Pressmen and photographers camped outside our house. In the end, I sent a friend back to the garage with the keys of my car, which he drove round the countryside for a couple of hours, followed by a convoy of vehicles, before leaving it parked outside the main station. We drove off to another retreat in Ray's car, leaving the Press besieging the station. A few days later, I arrived home to find a Political writer from the Daily Mail in the kitchen. He had charmed his way in by telling my daughters he had brought me some flowers, and was chatting away quite happily with them. I soon sent him on his way!

"I couldn't resist it, when some of the TV people asked me if I would like to appear in a play called 'Newshounds' which was all about a national tabloid. I had to be interviewed by a real bag of a woman columnist, who had the interview ruined for her by her photographer's constant interference. I loved every minute of it, because I felt I was getting a bit of my own back".

Forceful, unrepentant and energetic, Edwina Currie seems destined to go on making headlines, and probably achieving great things, for a good many years yet. She is one of Liverpool's most controversial and enterprising daughters, and few things would please her more than to see the city of her birth rise to greatness again. As she admits, she owes it a considerable debt, if only because its ill-disciplined vigour, irrepresible humour and sheer bloody-mindedness has helped to make her the dynamic woman she undoubtedly is.

Lord Derby

One Merseysider who has lived through more changes than most is the eighteenth Earl of Derby, grandson of a man who was, for many years, the close confidante of Royalty and widely known as the uncrowned King of Lancashire. Born in London at the end of World War 1, he spent much of his early childhood at the imposing ancestral home of Knowsley because, he says, it was generally felt healthier for children to be brought up in the fresh air of the countryside.

Even today, the great hall stands in more than 2,000 acres of parkland, with sheep and birds everywhere. Then, he recalls, it was possible to drive through the gates in a small dog cart, and travel a couple of miles before reaching the first house. "The area has become terribly built-up in recent years", he explains with understandable sadness. "People were moved out from Liverpool after the last war, and a great deal of land was taken for housing as well as for industry. It was all part of the process of rebuilding Liverpool after the bombing, and done with the best of motives, but I am not altogether sure, now, that it was the right thing to do. Long-standing communities were broken up, and I think the city itself has also suffered".

It was the gradual urbanisation of what had once been rolling country that pursuaded Lord Derby to embark on what was perhaps the most dramatic and unexpected project of his lifetime, the creation of a 360-acre Safari Park. Other great landowners had already opened their houses to the public or constructed large amusement areas, partly to offset mounting death duties and partly to provide alternative sources of income. Both considerations doubtless helped to influence His Lordship's thinking, but he is adamant that the main reason was a desire to preserve a sizeable open space or "lung" while there was still time.

"I felt it only right there should be somewhere that local people, or from further afield for that matter, could visit in their spare time", he says. "We had this area of land available and it seemed a sensible thing to do. Actually it wasn't quite such an innovation as you think, because one of my ancestors, the thirteenth earl, created what was then the largest zoo in Europe at the start of the nineteenth century. He was a great zoologist, who travelled abroad extensively, and he collected rare animals from all over the world.

"I suppose it wasn't a zoo in the modern sense, because it wasn't open to the public at large, but I imagine the local people were very much aware of it! It was apparently rather on the lines of Whipsnade, with the animals roaming about fairly freely, which was in itself a very progressive idea for the times. That zoo survived for 40-50 years, but the next earl was not so interested and most of the animals ended up as exhibits in Liverpool Museum".

To help him with the project, Lord Derby called on Jimmy Chipperfield of the famous circus family, who had already created wildlife parks at Woburn and Longleat and has long been associated with the Safari Park at Windsor. In 1971 the Knowsley Park was opened, with a flurry of trumpeting if not of trumpets, and the inhabitants of Knowsley were introduced to the unfamiliar sounds of an African Jungle.

"I am happy to say the whole thing has been an unqualified success, particularly since we said goodbye to the Chipperfields and decided to run the park ourselves", Lord Derby explains. "We had

Instead of Old Masters, tigers and elephants, Lord and Lady Derby with one of the younger inhabitants of the Knowsley Safari Park.

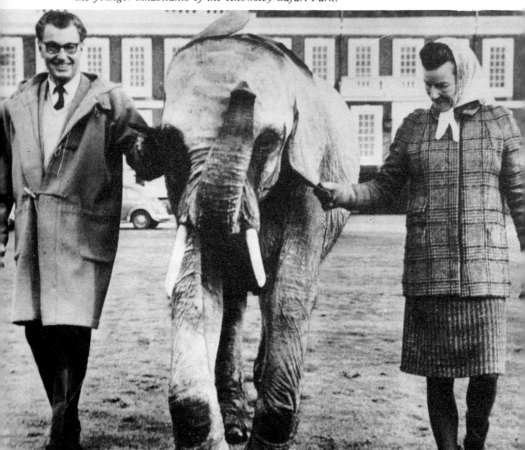

tremendous problems at first, as you invariably do when you venture into the unknown, but we learned from them, and I think we have got it pretty well right now. I don't run it myself, of course, there is a professional manager to do that, but I am fully involved, I take a close personal interest, and I do make all the major decisions.

"We started off with the biggest herd of elephants outside Africa, and they have remained extremely popular. The use of electric fences, which they learned to understand remarkably quickly, is a big help because visitors can approach quite close in complete safety and without having their view impaired. I think it is only when you get close to an elephant that you realise just how huge it is, and what a very impressive beast.

"Some of the other imports were not so successful. Lions have generally done very well (after all, they lived wild in Britain not so very long ago!) but neither giraffes nor hippos proved at all suitable and we have had to get rid of them. Giraffes need a great deal of open space, while hippos need plenty of deep, warm water and mud. In the early days we lost a few cheetahs, which was sad, but on the credit side we have brought in tigers which have done extraordinarily well. Funnily enough, the baboons seem to be the most popular with the visitors, even though they are liable to damage car aerials and windscreen wipers. I can't stand them myself, but there you are".

Financing such an ambitious project was not easy. Cost of the Safari Park was an estimated £750,000, and although the Derby's have always been great landowners, once owning much of Lancashire, the family are not industrial or commercial giants. To raise the necessary cash, Lord Derby was forced to sell a number of well-known paintings, including a Van Dyke hanging in Liverpool's Walker Art Gallery which fetched some £400,000. Also sold were a set of Elizabethan miniatures, including one of Sir Francis Drake, and a set of botanical books, as the Earl adopted the essentially pragmatic approach of looking forward rather than back.

In that he was following the example of his ancestors. Lord Thomas Stanley, who won the original earldom by the perfect timing of his arrival at Bosworth Field more than 500 years ago, would surely have applauded the enterprise of the present Earl in demonstrating his willingness to move with the times. Lord Thomas' zeal in raising armies for various national causes was matched by his skill in bringing them to the field of battle just as victory was assured, and the opportunism that led him to seize the crown as it lay beneath a thorn bush and thrust it upon Henry Tudor's head.

"He was a clever fellow with a great political awareness", says the present earl. "In those days if you backed the wrong side, you ended up losing your head. Most of the great families who have survived have had to steer a pretty careful course and ours is no exception. Of course times have changed a great deal in recent years, but it remains just as important to continue looking ahead rather than living in the past.

"So far as the Safari Park is concerned, we have made a good many changes since we took over ourselves. The Chipperfields believed in leaving the animals out all year and keeping the park open most of the time. We now keep them inside in bad weather, and close the park altogether. The result has been a dramatic fall in the number of deaths and much more consistent breeding. The animals generally seem much happier, and I think that shows itself in their appearance and behaviour. We have been voted the best Safari Park in Britain, and we have an excellent relationship with the zoos in Chester and Whipsnade, which means we can always help each other. We probably benefit from being the only large park in the North, and we got a valuable boost when we were involved in an episode of Coronation Street! Some people raised their eyebrows when we opened, but I believe Merseyside would miss the Safari Park quite badly now if it had to close".

Strictly speaking, Lord Derby is not a Liverpudlian. He has always thought of himself as a Lancastrian, but grew up in an age when both Liverpool and Manchester were part of the larger county, and still feels municipal reorganisation was a bad mistake. "I suppose it may have been necessary for administrative purposes, but I have found most people only too happy to think of themselves as Lancastrians, particularly in the field of sport", he admits. "The family estates are in Lancashire, but we have always had a close personal involvement with Liverpool. In fact my grandfather was once Lord Mayor. Incidentally, I am delighted the City Council has decided to re-establish that position, because I think it can be a valuable source of prestige.

"The lady who filled the post initially, Councillor Dorothy Gavin, did a splendid job for Liverpool, and I am sure it strengthened her hand when she was introduced as Lord Mayor rather than just Chairman of the Council. Really, it just underlines the sadness of what has happened in local government in recent years. I used to sit on Lancashire County Council, before I became Lord Lieutenant, and some of my best friends were socialists. In the old days, people of different persuasions belonged to different parties, but they had an overriding loyalty to the county, and were not always carrying out party policy, often decided from outside.

"I came back onto the County Council after finishing my term as Lord Lieutenant, but everything had changed by then. We no longer had the aldermen, who used to do a valuable job and brought a great deal of experience with them. They might have started out as extreme right-wingers or left-wing socialists, but by then they had invariably mellowed and acted as elder statesmen capable of deciding an issue on its merits. I think the country lost a great deal when the office of alderman was abolished.

"So far as Liverpool is concerned, I have only looked on from the outside, politically, but I used to have a great deal of respect for people like the Braddocks who did their best for everyone and tried hard to help the city recover from the damage done during the war. I think a great deal of harm has been done in other ways by what has seemed to be constant in-fighting, but it does look as though things are beginning to settle down again at last. Liverpool has had a hard time, partly because it has attracted such a bad Press, and it is vital that everyone pulls together now".

Lord Derby may not have had a close political involvement with Liverpool, but his life and his career have had a strong Liverpool flavour. A career soldier with the Grenadier Guards, who reached the rank of major, won the Military Cross, and was invalided home after the Battle of Anzio, he was only allowed to resign his Regular Commission on condition that he agreed to become colonel of the 5th King's (Liverpool) Territorial Regiment. "When it became clear I was needed at home, I had to quit the Army and study finance and administration in London, before returning to Knowsley", he explains. "I was sorry at the time, because I enjoyed soldiering, but it was clear I would soon have to take over the family estates so I needed to be able to read a balance sheet. The Territorials were an important part of the nation's defences, but it was terribly hard to find recruits, because so many people who had been serving in the forces didn't want any further involvement. Funnily enough, a large number of our recruits were ex-sailors".

Just to demonstrate lack of bias, Lord Derby also became an honorary captain in the Mersey Division of the R.N.R., and he has held a number of other posts in and around the city. One of the most important is that of President of the Merseyside Chamber of Commerce, a body which, with the help of Lord Leverhulme, he did much to establish. "The individual chambers had done a great deal to promote trade, particularly in the field of export, but they lacked the muscle to make a significant impact", he says. "We felt a combined chamber could speak for the area as a whole, because Merseyside really does need all the friends outside that it can get. The success of

A man of many talents. Lord Derby in his uniform of Hon. Captain of the Mersey branch of the R.N.V.R.

the many trade missions that Merseyside has mounted abroad speaks for itself. By combining our resources we greatly increase our influence".

Another major involvement has been with the world-famous area of Aintree. "I remember, when I was on the County Council many years ago, the chairman came up to me in the corridor one day and asked me: "Do you know anything about this piece of land?"", he recalls. "He said that some unfortunate little woman was losing a lot of money and wanted to develop the land, and did I think that would be all right?

"I realised he was talking about Aintree Racecourse and Mrs Topham. He asked me to come with him to meet her, and she told us a wonderful sob story about how the Grand National was finished, because she had tried everything and the public just didn't want to know. I said: 'Mrs

Topham, can you put your hand on your heart and say with all honesty that you are not making at least £50,000 a year? She replied: 'What has that got to do with it! I don't think I should have to answer that question', and I replied: 'How about £60,000 or even £70,000?' She wouldn't answer, for the very good reason that she knew she was making a very healthy profit, but had seen the chance to make a lot more through commercial development.

"Of course she didn't get planning permission, so she tried all sorts of different approaches instead. She may have been a remarkable character, with a great deal of individuality, but I shall never believe she was terribly interested in either Aintree Racecourse or the Grand National. As you know, there was a great deal of trouble after that, and we have all had to fight extremely hard to save what is a part of our national heritage. I agreed to become a Trustee of the Appeal because I felt it would be dreadful if Merseyside was to lose such a wonderful asset".

Although the Derby Family home is only round the corner from Aintree, and many of the 18 earls, including the present one, have ridden over fences when young, their traditional racing involvement has always been with the Flat, especially since a past Lord Derby gave his name to the most famous flat race in the world. However, the present Lord Derby remains an Aintree steward, and has attended the race and enjoyed its thrills and spills since an early age.

"As a child, I can remember King George V and Queen Mary staying with us at Knowsley, and then paying a private visit to the National", he says. "Being very young, I was kept well out of the way most of the time, and had to be on my best behaviour. Some kind of entertainment was invariably laid on for the benefit of the Royal guests, and this led to one or two embarrassing moments.

"One year the two comedians, George Formby and George Robey, were invited to appear, and the latter got rather carried away. He was sitting next to the King, and when George Formby told a very funny joke, he roared with laughter, dug the King in the ribs with his elbow and shouted out, 'Nice one, George!' Nobody was quite sure which George he meant, but neither the King nor Queen Mary was amused.

"Another incident was even worse. The famous French boxer Georges Carpentier had been invited to Knowsley to give an exhibition against a comparative unknown, and of course he was always a perfect gentleman and very well behaved. At one time the exhibition was going to be held in the drawing room, and although it was switched to the stables, Queen Mary decided she would attend,

A regular host to Royalty. Lord Derby at Aintree with a radiant young Queen Elizabeth 2 and the Queen Mother.

which was extremely daring of her at that time. Unfortunately the boxer who had been found to oppose Carpentier was either unfit, drunk or both. Every time Carpentier hit him, which was fairly frequently, he either let out a belch, spat on the floor, or swore. On a couple of occasions he even vomitted in front of the Queen. There was a dreadful row afterwards and everyone was full of apologies".

In later years, after Lord Derby had left the Army, inherited the Earldom and moved into Knowsley Hall, members of the Royal Family continued to be frequent visitors. "We entertained most of them at one time or another", he remembers. "King George VI came with Queen Elizabeth, now the Queen Mother, as well as the present Queen and Princess Margaret. It used to be an annual visit until the tragedy of Devon Loch. I still don't know what happened then, but I have never heard a noise like it on a racecourse before or since, as the large crowd prepared to welcome a Royal winner. It is possible that affected the horse.

"Of course I used to entertain them in my role of Lord Lieutenant, and as we still lived at Knowsley Hall, there was plenty of room. Nowadays I no longer live in the Hall because it was much too big, and I am no longer Lord Lieutenant, though obviously I retain my interest in the racing. It is good to see the crowds at Aintree growing bigger each year, and to hear that we are to have a second meeting in the autumn. It is a further indication of the way people here are learning to live with changing times and, on the whole, doing so successfully".

It must have taken a considerable personal adjustment for Lord Derby to fit into his present environment, which is both smaller and less grand than the setting he was originally accustomed to. When he married Lady Isabel Milles-Cade (who died in 1990) at Westminster Abbey in 1948, the ceremony was attended by the entire Royal Family, and he returned home to a residence that had once employed some 50 servants. "I suppose I was sorry to give it up in one way", he admits, "but it was much too large for us, and horribly expensive. Even the New House that I had built was really bigger than we needed, and I was glad to see the Hall put to good use.

"The County Police used part of it for a time, and now Merseyside Police have moved in instead. Understandably, it is useful for them to have the use of a large building well away from everything else, so it has been a good arrangement. The main public rooms are let out for conferences and the occasional major function, which is handy again because there are not too many places around which can offer so much space. I have had requests to let the hall be used for the occasional ball or social function, but nothing is allowed to carry on late at night for obvious security reasons".

The New House, a pleasant residence looking out over the lake, would seem very large for most of us but is extremely modest by Knowsley standards. Lord Derby's study has a pleasant informality about it, as he sits there with a couple of his dogs, a large black labrador which insists on barking at regular intervals, and a much smaller Jack Russell, which leaps up in desperate protest every time his Lordship breaks off to feed a hen pheasant and her chicks beneath the window.

Over the fireplace there hangs a familiar-looking painting which turns out to be a Stubbs. "We found it in the servants' hall when we were clearing out during the move", says Lord Derby. "It was black and unrecognisable, but as soon as I had a good look I was sure what it was, and so I had it cleaned. Stubbs used to work here for a time, you know. In the old days there was usually a resident painter at Knowsley, it was a kind of sponsorship I suppose, and Stubbs came when a man called Winstanley was in residence. Winstanley soon realised the new man was better than him and sent him on his way, but he did paint a few pictures while he was at Knowsley, and this is one of them. It's nice to have it here as a personal memento.

"I don't know if you realised it, but Edward Lear lived here too, in much the same way. My ancestor saw him painting birds at London Zoo and invited him to come and paint some at Knowsley instead. He used to have tea with the children in the schoolroom. One afternoon Lady Derby asked why the children stayed up there instead of joining the rest of the family and was told it was because of 'The funny man who writes such amusing verses'. She went upstairs herself, was delighted with his poetry, and did a great deal to make sure it reached a much wider public. Most of his poems are in fact dedicated to the Derby Children".

Mention of Stubbs is a reminder of Lord Derby's racing connections. The family have always been associated with the turf, have owned many famous winners including the great Derby and St. Leger winner Hyperium in 1933, and still have a home at Newmarket, though they sold the famous Stanley House Stables way back in 1978. "I had 28 horses in training once upon a time, but there are only 10 now, and only three of them have actually run", says Lord Derby rather wistfully. "I remember once having four winners in a row at Haydock, all ridden by Doug Smith. The last one was quoted at 3-1 in the morning, but by the time it actually ran it was 100-7 on. I believe the bookmakers took quite a caning.

"The last major success I had came with Teleprompter, which Bill Watts trained to win the 1975 Budweiser Million in Chicago. He was a great big gelding, and so frisky that the Americans christened him Rambo, though he was as gentle as a child really. I did have high hopes of his half-brother Message Pad, but so far he has been very disappointing. The cost of racing is going up all the time, and it is becoming increasingly hard to compete with the Arabs because they can afford to pay such high prices. You have seen what has happened to Robert Sangster since he tried to compete, and there is certainly no way that I can".

Opposite:
A rider as well as a racehorse owner. Lord Derby in point-to-point action in his younger days.

Ken Dodd

If it is true that you have to be a comedian to survive in Liverpool, then nothing could me more appropriate than for Ken Dodd to be uncrowned King of Knotty Ash. No one person is better liked or respected in the city despite his recent brush with the Inland Revenue. None conveys better that feeling of wry amusement at the state of society mingled with a certain pathos, that is so typical of modern Merseyside. That he has become extremely rich over the years, both before and after satisfying the demands of the Tax inspector, is immaterial. Like many other self-made men, money has become relatively unimportant to him for its own sake, though he has had to work hard enough for it to insist that he is paid the rate for the job.

The cosmopolitan atmosphere of Merseyside may be responsible for the fact that it has produced more entertainers, musicians and comedians than any other city in the British Isles. Merely looking towards the makers of mirth, one recalls Tommy Handley, who held a war-ravaged nation spellbound with his weekly series ITMA, Rob Wilton, Ted Ray, Arthur Askey, Derek Guyler and, more recently, Jimmy Tarbuck, Stan Boardman and Tom O'Connor. All of them established a nationwide reputation for humour, yet none was so closely identified with Liverpool, its problems and its triumphs as Ken Dodd, who has gradually become part of its folk lore, an essential piece of the fabric of the place.

That is not to say his appeal has ever been parochial. He has enjoyed smash hits in such varied places as the London Palladium, Bournemouth, Buxton and, of course, Liverpool Empire, proving equally popular with pensioners, teenagers and the middle-aged, and with millionaires, Royalty and the unemployed. Like all the best entertainers, his style is classless and sexless — despite the numerous innuendos and double-entendres of which he is so fond, yet throughout a long and varied career he has never been taken for anything but a distinguished representative of the city that gave him birth, and which has enjoyed his relentless progress to the top with much personal pride.

Whole books have been written about 'Doddy's' individual brand of humour, which has been analysed, discussed and classified by numerous theatrical critics. I do not claim to know him well enough to attempt my own definition, but there has to be a lot of the professional clown in his approach, which depends so much on exploitation of the ridiculous, as personified by his own appearance. The protruding teeth, the spiky, stand-up strands of hair, the garish suits and the ever-present Tickling Stick have all become essential parts of his equipment, which have helped to keep audiences laughing from the moment he bounces on stage. And in this emphasis on the ridiculous, this constant reminder of the funny side of human frailty, one senses a deep, inbred empathy with the common man and woman, the ordinary, cheerful, under-priviledged inhabitant of our teeming inner-cities who has helped to make Britain what it is.

Anyone who has ever enjoyed a drink in a Liverpool pub, or one in Birmingham, Newcastle or Leeds for that matter, or who has ever stood on the Anfield Kop will know what I mean. When human nature is brought together in the mass, as it was in the wartime air-raid shelter with which Ken Dodd soon grew familiar, and as it is in the busy back street of a big city, a certain communal warmth, kindled by spontaneous wit, emerges to bind even the most humble together. It has been Ken Dodd's special skill that he has been able to share this special communal feeling, and understand intuitively what is likely to appeal to the mass of an audience.

That does not mean, of course, that 'Doddy' is one of those spontaneous, off-the-cuff comics who make up their jokes as they go along. He is and always has been far too professional for that. No man has worked harder, with expert assistance, to obtain first class material, to rehearse its application or to study what jokes, what sudden asides and even what songs obtain the best response. His memory is legendary in the business, but that memory is invariably reinforced by carefully prepared aids which help to ensure that every utterance is apt, topical, delivered with confidence and well-timed. As they say in most kinds of sport, the true professional is the man who can make what he does look easy. The real measure of Ken Dodd's supreme professionalism is that he frequently looks as though he is simply enjoying an extremely lively night out with a number of old friends.

As I have already said, Ken Dodd's roots are deep-set in Liverpool and seem likely to stay there. He still lives in the large, but far from ostentatious former farm house in Thomas Lane where he was born way back in 1927, and unlike most famous men is happy to play a modest part in the local community. He has not bought a handsome residence on the banks of the Thames, established a second home in some posh tax haven like Bermuda or the Isle of Man, or surrounded himself with Minders and barbed wire. He continues to exchange jokes with the postman and milkman, to open the occasional church fete, to answer telephone calls personally (after they have been taken on an answering machine) and to make it clear that so far as he is concerned, Liverpool is very much his spiritual home.

Much of this may be due to his upbringing by parents who also had their roots in the community, his father being a coal merchant who was also a part-time musician. And from his early days it is clear he was a happy child as well as one with a strong sense of humour. When he jokes: "I was a very happy baby", he is probably doing no more than telling the truth, and certainly one of the reasons for his phenominal success is that he has always put the emphasis on happiness, urging his audiences to excercise their "chuckle-muscles" and even employing a ballad entitled "Happiness, the greatest gift that I possess" as his theme song. People spending hard-earned money on a rare night out with their family and friends, could hardly ask for a better guarantee of pleasure, particularly if seeking to overcome the trauma of personal sadness or unemployment.

Such personal happiness even survived its share of hardship, for Dodd's parents were not especially well off. "Every Christmas Eve we would go to bed and my father was still out trying to sell coal after midnight", he recalls. "In those days people would get their coal in during the week and pay whenever you could catch them in. My mother would start collecting money on a Thursday, when some people had been paid, and she would be out from the afternoon until 11 o'clock in the evening. On Saturdays she would set off from Knotty Ash about nine in the morning and return home just before midnight. She would get a tram back from Prescot having walked all the way collecting money. It was dangerous carrying money in a handbag and once she was set upon and robbed by four men. Mum was 5ft 1in tall".

Somehow or other the very name of Knotty Ash seems appropriate for a comedian who likes to call his house Doddy Towers, and has endowed the area with a mythical group of 'Jam-butty mines'. Like Fazackerley, another Liverpool district with an extraordinary title, Knotty Ash conjures up an image of pantomime, the sort of place where one would expect to come across a host of 'Diddymen' playing strange musical instruments and performing highly unusual feats. Although he has no children and appears to live as conventional a home life as is possible with his seemingly endless commitments, it is hard to avoid the conclusion that in Dodd's case, reality and fantasy are never far apart. Certainly he gives the impression when playing in pantomime or some other large stage production that he inevitably allows to over-run for up to half-an-hour at a time, that in a very real sense, the stage is not so much his second as his first and true home.

It is widely known that Ken Dodd's father encouraged him to play a wide variety of musical instruments, though at that time they did not include the huge drum he now bangs with such relish, and to join

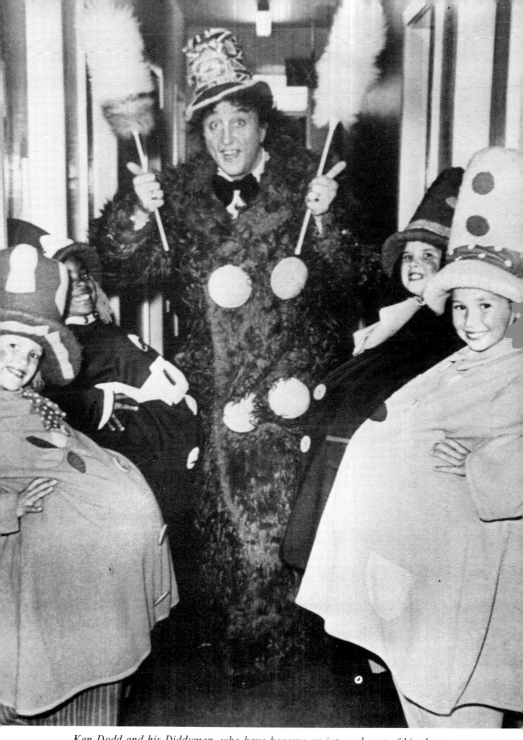

Ken Dodd and his Diddymen, who have become an integral part of his show.

33

the St. John's Church choir, where he first discovered that he had a melodious and tuneful voice. With such support it is hardly surprising he developed into an entertainer, though it was an advertisement in the Liverpool Echo for a booklet on "How to become a ventriloquist" that really started him off. With his little doll Charlie Brown he gave his first public performance at St. Edward's Orphanage at the age of eight, including tap dancing and tunes on both piano and saxophone along with his ventriliquist act in the repertoire.

Such virtuosity brought its proper reward. After the concert, the Father Superior sent for the young prodigy who recalls: "I thought I was going to get a good hiding for being a rotten ventriloquist. Instead, he gave me half-a-crown". Later he performed for the school's parent-teachers association, and was rewarded with a shilling. "I had to learn my first lesson in show business — how to take a cut gracefully", he jokes. "I did a show at the Scala at the age of ten and played the Philharmonic Hall when I was twelve. Wherever there was an audience, I would be there with my suitcase and my props. The case was bigger than me. My father's advice was I must be original and have my own style, and I always tried to do that. The basic philosophy from my mother was that you can do anything you want to do, and be anybody you want to be — if you try hard enough".

Considering his early start, it seems a little surprising that Ken Dodd did not turn professional until he was 27, a good 10 years after he left school (Holt H.S.) for the last time. He helped his father with the coal business, then ran his own mobile shop, all the while continuing to gain theatrical experience through appearing at pubs, clubs and after dinner engagements. Always he was learning, notably what made people laugh, and picking up what he could from established performers. In the end, it took the combined efforts of agent Dave Forrester, who actually sought him out, and Anne Boutin, the lady who was to become his secretary and fiancee for so many eventful years, to persuade him that he was ready for a full time theatrical career.

In view of his strong Liverpudlian connection, it is interesting to note that Ken Dodd made his professional debut in variety at the Empire Theatre, Nottingham in September 1954 on a bill that also featured singer Tony Brent, trumpeter Kenny Baker and the Kordites. He was a reasonable success, and was soon making further appearances in Leeds, Manchester, Sunderland and Colwyn Bay. While at Colwyn Bay, he was spotted by B.B.C. producer Barney Colehan, who featured him in the televised production of the Good

Old Days at the Leeds Empire, for the princely fee of £32 9s 2d. From then on, the Liverpool comedian was on the way to the stars.

A series of short — for him — appearances on Workers Playtime announced his arrival on radio, and confirmed his ability to overwhelm an audience with a staccato series of jokes and funny remarks, delivered at such speed that it was hard to catch all of them, which was to become one of his trademarks. Another, which has delighted audiences but frustrated producers throughout his life, is his inability to stop. Producer Jim Casey recalls seeing Dodd entertain factory workers for 20 minutes at a time, after his Workers Playtime performances had finished, and commented: "All he wanted was an audience, the location was not important". Even then, Casey thought that Ken Dodd was 'obsessed with comedy, and would perform even if he was not paid for it". Little has changed in the intervening years. As audiences at concerts, music halls and celebrity dinners know full well, once Ken Dodd is launched into his comedy routine he is liable to carry on long after the last bus has gone and the waiters have started to go home.

A great asset, especially in his early days, was Dodd's association with another distinguished Liverpudlian, script writer Eddie Braben. A former barrow boy in Liverpool's St. John's Market, and another man of the people, Braben was just the person to produce raw material for the up and coming comedian, who liked to tell so many gags that he needed a regular supply. At that time, Dodd was mostly concerned with straight joke-telling, so it hardly mattered that Braben had little experience of writing comedy sketches, but the pair of them soon expanded their horizons as their joint careers began to take off.

In 1956, Dodd achieved two major ambitions. The first was topping the bill in his own home town theatre, the Liverpool Empire, with a cast that included Jimmy James; the second, appearing at Blackpool at the same time as Morecombe and Wise and helping the Central Pier Pavilion break all box office records. Inevitably, his show frequently over-ran the time allowed, but none of the holiday-makers who staggered out afterwards, holding their sides, were going to complain about that. Already, after a comparatively short public exposure, he was beginning to be accepted as a major public figure, one of the up-and-coming generation of first class entertainers who were to dominate the sixties and seventies.

Typically, Ken Dodd preferred to return home after each show, rather than spend time fraternising with friends and fellow performers in Blackpool. Even then he was, as he still is, a very private person who likes to sit down in peace and quiet to discuss his performance with a friend or friends. Probably too, he knew he could rely on his parents and Anne Boutin for a realistic assessment of his performance that would be of more value than the uncontrolled adulation of little-known admirers. For a comedian, like a footballer or a politician, is only as good as his last performance. Reputation alone counts for little if an act begins to lose its magic, and Dodd was determined that he would never fail through taking anything for granted. Instead, he worked ever harder to extend and perfect his act, striving for perfection, if such a thing is possible in Show Business, and adding the singing of an occasional sentimental ballad to his repertoire. Although he soon realised he was not cut out to be an opera singer, he knew that a well sung song helped to break up his programme and went down exceptionally well with the ladies.

Always Dodd was working, and planning and experimenting, while Anne Boutin helped him keep a remarkable record of audience reaction at every performance. Although apparently convulsed with laughter on stage he was practical, efficient and highly professional off it, approaching comedy in the scientific manner of a university researcher determined to accept nothing without firm evidence. Wisely, he realised that jokes which would paralyse a Liverpudlian or a Yorkshireman with mirth might not go down as well in Scotland or, above all in London, which he knew he had to conquer if he wanted to become a personality of truly national stature.

That was, of course, helped considerably by his continued success on both radio and television, success that owed much to his sheer force of personality, since he found it almost impossible to keep within prescribed time limits. But he was in no hurry. "I can't say I like the West End scene", he told a friend in the late fifties. "It scares me a bit. Everybody's so reserved and tight-lipped. They remind me of those characters in a bad gangster film who hate each other. It's different back in Liverpool". It certainly was. Over Christmas 1963 his home town audience sold out the Royal Court and loved every minute of a show wrapped in Beatlemania, during which 'Ringo' Dodd leaped out on stage clutching an enormous guitar.

It was April 1965 before Doddy appeared at the London Palladium but when he did he took the place by storm, as he has continued to do on his appearances there ever since. For his London

Opposite:
Not just a comedian, more an all-round entertainer. Ken Dodd shows off the Golden Disc awarded him for his ballad "Tears".

act he had cut out a few Merseyside references which he knew would not be understood, but in all other respects he was the typical Liverpool comedian. The Palladium's Leslie McDonnell, later confessed to serious doubts about whether Dodd's North Country accent and humour would be acceptable, but he need not have worried. Both houses were sold out on the first night, both performances over-ran, and the evening ended in the happiest of chaos. In the words of the show's title "Doddy's Here", and for most of the 5,000 plus present, that was quite sufficient. Old hands said they had never seen anything like the enthusiasm engendered, and the critics of the National Press concurred with that judgement. "Ken Dodd wins the Cockneys" was just one of the many blazing headlines that greeted his London triumph the following morning.

Playwright John Osborne wrote: "We went away from the Palladium exhilerated and awed by this incredible phenomenon of human invention and overwhelming energy".

The London Palladium appearance confirmed Dodd's arrival as a genuine super star, and suddenly everything was running for him. Ballads like 'The River' and 'Tears' were topping the Hit Parade, attracting even more attention than 'Love is Like a Violin' had done, he was in constant demand for shows on both radio and television and he was even signed up to top the bill at the Royal Variety Show. The funny man from Knotty Ash had joined the ranks of the elite. Many, many celebrities in a similar situation would have torn up their roots and moved into fashionable society, buying big cars, playing celebrity golf at the weekend and returning home only for well publicised visits to boost tour attendances. Not Ken Dodd. He remained very much his own man, not even buying a bigger car, and remaining loyal to his native city, his family and his friends.

When his local M.P. Prime Minister Harold Wilson, turned up at the Palladium with his family and Liverpool firebrand Bessie Braddock, Ken Dodd's cup of joy was full to overflowing. He welcomed them with enthusiasm, cracked tasteful jokes at their expense and thanked them for coming. Though a staunch Conservative himself, who believes in free enterprise, he was delighted that a man he greatly respected should recognise just what he had achieved. The comedian from Knotty Ash may have become an international star overnight and assured himself of many future bookings in the nation's finest theatres, but he had the sense to know the importance of retaining a stable base in his home town. It was perhaps symbolic of his attitude that he even had a photograph of the Liverpool Footbal Club's team pasted on the wall of the famous No. 1 dressing room.

"Some have greatness thrust upon them." Ken Dodd as he appeared as Malvolio in the Liverpool production of Shakespeare's Twelfth Night.

Once started, the Ken Dodd bandwagon has rolled on and on. Variety, pantomime, a one man marathon 'Mirthquake' at Liverpool's Royal Court, a whole series of shows at the Palladium, the last one as recently as 1990, and of course regular appearances on both television and radio, as well as numerous bookings at clubs and dinners. The man's energy and his appetite for comedy has been well nigh insatiable. Arguments still rage as to whether Dodd is as funny on television as he is on stage, and certainly the small box tends to subdue his ebullient personality, but the public at large remain switched on. Even when he made a rare excursion into serious acting to play Malvolio in a memorable production of Twelfth Night at Liverpool Playhouse, both audience and critics loved him, amazed that he could switch so effortlessly (or so it seemed) from one form of theatrical entertainment to another.

In later years he has had to withstand his share of knocks. The tragic death of Anne Boutin through cancer in 1976 hit him badly, and there were even suggestions he might retire, though that never seemed likely given his obsession for the stage. Then, much more recently, came his encounter with the Inland Revenue, which to the disbelief of his millions of admirers, threatened to destroy him completely. Suddenly, one of the nation's favourite people, a comedian who had given enormous entertainment for more than 30 years and campaigned successfully to save at least three theatres from closure was seemingly threatened with the possibility of being sent to prison. It seemed unthinkable, particularly as Dodd, for all his earnings, has never coveted possessions and lived a remarkably simple life stripped of luxuries.

The trial, immensely painful and embarrassing for an essentially private person, revealed a good deal about the kind of man he is. He was shown to be a simple, rather old-fashioned person, almost Victorian in his distrust of bookkeeping and banks, thrifty and strangely fearful, for one so successful, of a day when he might no longer be earning large sums of money. He was shown to have made "cash and carry" flights to the Isle of Man to deposit money there in the belief it was not liable to tax, and to have hidden large sums in the roof of his house because he feared the outbreak of civil war. Even more surprisingly Dodd revealed he had not been on holiday until he reached the age of 51, and had gone up to three years without buying a new suit.

As his Q.C. Mr George Carman emphasised, Ken Dodd "has lived in a world of fantasy, a world, on occasion, of folly and a world of insecurity, His conduct, so obviously eccentric, is to be explained, not by dishonesty but by the close-knit family upbringing of which he was so much a part for most of his adult life. It was an upbringing which stamped on him the virtues of another age, thrift, relentless hard work, close family loyalty and great charity for others. Money is not the beginning and the end of Ken Dodd. Far from it". Ken Dodd himself described the motivation which has driven him on as follows: "I didn't want a Rolls Royce or a villa or a big house with a swimming pool. The one thing I wanted most in life was to be a star and get to the Palladium and prove to my family that I could be someone. It was positive proof that I was a star — to have that nest egg".

When the jury eventually found Dodd not guilty, he was free to pick up the threads of his life again, although it must have taken a great deal of doing. The long trial, and perhaps even worse the period leading up to it, had left him badly shaken and for a time he seemed to have aged and lost some of his natural zest for life. But with his good friend Sybil Anne Jones to help him, and a sympathetic Liverpool public to boost his morale, it was not long before he was as chirpy as ever. For a man in his sixties, it was a phenominal performance, because as anyone who has ever seen him in action knows, Ken Dodd probably expends more nervous energy in a single performance than the average First Division footballer does in a whole season.

A child of Merseyside, he clearly has the Merseysiders' natural resilience, a resilience that enabled them to survive even the Blitz and still emerge laughing afterwards. In a city famous for its fiddles and its permissive attitude to many aspects of law breaking, Ken Dodd would not have lacked friends even if he had been found guilty of tax evasion. But the real reason for the widespread support and sympathy he received, both before and after the trial, had nothing to do with that. It was due to the realisation that here is a basically good, kind man who has devoted his life to making other people happy and persuading them to laugh. Not a bad qualification to be numbered among the great Liverpudlians.

Harold Francis

It is quite possible that few people outside Merseyside (and not all within the area) are familiar with the name of Harold Hugh Francis, but this quietly-spoken medical man with the New Zealand accent has made as profound an impact on its life as any other single person over the last 20 or 30 years. For Mr Francis, an internationally recognised gynaecologist and obstetrician, has led a world-wide campaign against over-population which has saved thousands of mothers from poverty and over-exhaustion, and prevented many unwanted children from being born.

Entering the world shortly before Christmas, 1918 in the little Dorset town of Sturminster, Harold Francis emigrated to New Zealand with his recently widowed mother at the tender age of three, and was brought up in that country. He took his B.Sc. at the University of New Zealand in 1939, gained general medical qualifications four years later and worked as a house surgeon at hospitals in both Dunedin and Wellington, before winning an advanced post-graduate scholarship in obstetrics and gynaecology offered by the University of Otago in 1946. "That gave me entry into the Women's Hospitals at Melbourne and Sydney and decided the direction of my future career", he points out. "At that time I never had any doubt that I would make my career in that part of the world, and I only came to England to widen my experience, gain extra qualifications and earn a little more money. Things were pretty tight in both Australia and New Zealand at the time, and I've never seen so many starving gynaecologists in my life. Local doctors tended to hold on to their own patients as long as they could, and many small private hospitals were forced to close.

"Eventually I landed a job as house surgeon and Registrar at Leicester Royal Infirmary and worked there for four years, gaining my first English qualification (F.R.C.S.) just four days before the Coronation. I've always been a great admirer of the Monarchy and I was lucky enough to get a seat just outside the Abbey, but it seemed a mixed blessing at the time. It poured with rain all day and I was soaked through, so that every time I moved the water sloshed around inside my clothes. My lasting memory of the day wasn't of the Queen at all. It was of Queen Salote of Tonga beaming at us as she rode past in the rain in an open carriage. She must have been nearly as wet as me".

Harold Francis' arrival in Liverpool came almost entirely by chance. "I had been meaning to return home, because there was talk

of opening a big new maternity department, but nothing came of it",
he recalls. "I hung on in England, doing locum work, and then I was
tipped-off by an old friend, Jim Barr at Walton Hospital, that there
was a vacancy for a senior registrar at Liverpool Maternity Hospital
in Oxford Street. I applied and managed to pip a South African for
the job. Needless to say I was pleased, but I didn't expect to stay more
than two or three years, and if anyone had told me I would still be
working there in the 1990s I would have burst out laughing".

One reason for the lengthy stay was devotion to duty, with the new
arrival finding a desperate need for improved maternity care. The
other was his encounter with another member of staff, the middle
registrar, who just happened to be a lady and whom he married in
1955. "I suppose it was rather unique", he admits. "The two of us
working side by side in the same hospital for so many years. I was
number two to the great Professor (Sir Norman) Jeffcoate, and
Winifred (his wife) worked alongside him for more than 20 years.

"It was just as well we got on so perfectly together, because for the
first eight or nine years I must have been the busiest man in the North
West. I was in charge of a third of the beds at Oxford Street plus
numerous beds elsewhere, and on top of that I had to do a great deal
of Professor Jeffcoate's lecturing and teaching work, because he was
constantly away on tours to other parts of the world.

"Liverpool has always had something of a reputation for its
maternity care, and Professor Jeffcoate was the third Liverpudlian to
become President of the Royal College of Obstetricians and
Gynaecologists after Sir Arthur Gemmell and Professor Blair Bell,
who helped to found the college. Professor Jeffcoate was also the
Regional Assessor of Maternity Deaths, and I am proud to say that I
succeeded him when he retired in 1972. From then on, I was
responsible for examining the cause of death of every women in the
North of England, who died within a year of giving birth, and I can
tell you that is quite a responsibility".

Once established in Liverpool, Harold Francis became an ever
stronger advocate of birth control. "It was soon obvious to me that
Liverpool's high birth rate, then nearly a third above the national
average, was largely responsible for the high incidence of poverty in
the city", he explains. "At that time abortion was illegal, and by far
the most frequent cause of female deaths in pregnancy was back
street abortion. There were some terrifying cases which you would
hardly credit in today's more enlightened atmosphere. It was like
some foul game, and we couldn't interfere until the victims were
already seriously ill. All the perverts and weirdos had a free hand.

A world leader in the campaign for better birth control. Liverpool gynaechologist Harold Francis.

"There was one case of a woman abortionist who used a chromium-plated bicycle spoke to perform so-called operations, pushing it up through the cervix. It makes you sick just to think of it, but incidents like that were not all that uncommon. And because of the law, the victims were also open to blackmail.

"I remember one poor woman, quite well off and a pillar of the local church, going to see an abortionist, who walked off with her fur and her radio in addition to her agreed fee. She told the victim she didn't mind being prosecuted, because she already had a criminal record, but that the publicity would be degrading for the victim. Fortunately the lady concerned showed a lot of courage and insisted on prosecution, but obviously plenty of others before her had been too frightened to do so.

"Thank Heavens the Abortion Act went through in 1968, much to my surprise, I must admit. I am not a particular admirer of David Steel, but I think society in general owes him an enormous debt of gratitude for that action alone. Before the Act was passed, criminal abortion was the biggest single cause of maternal death, yet between 1982-84 there was not one single death from that cause. The figures speak for themselves.

"The move towards hospital deliveries has also helped to make maternity much safer as well as more comfortable. Way back in the fifties, a majority of deliveries in Liverpool at least, took place at home or in tiny little natal units. Our research showed that was very dangerous, but there seemed to be a prejudice against going into hospital. Fortunately the Government moved to encourage hospital births, and provided the finance to make them possible, and I'm happy to say that more than 90 per cent of deliveries take place in hospital today. In Liverpool's case, it led to a slight waste of money, because we had 37 domiciliary midwives, who were no longer really needed, but at least they provided valuable back-up immediately after birth".

In those early days, Mr Francis' work was almost entirely preventative, but as he became more familiar with Liverpool and its problems he began to move onto the offensive. "Anyone who takes the trouble to look around them and think must appreciate the dangers posed by over-population", he says. "The problem is world-wide, but initially I was just concerned for the women of Liverpool, many of whom were having far more children than they wanted or could hope to support. Believe it or not, in the 1950s and 1960s there were some women who had more children than they had menstrual periods. They did not practice birth control, either from ignorance or for religious reasons, and spent most of their adult lives trying to bring up children they did not want and could not provide for properly.

"Unfortunately our social benefits system encouraged people to have children for the wrong reasons. I have no doubt at all that many women, both in Liverpool and elsewhere, have given birth to children simply so that they will qualify for Council housing or other benefits. Society cannot cope with that situation and I have done my best to counter it.

"If there is one thing I would like to be remembered for, it is as the person who brought tubal ligation to the North West. When I came here, that particular form of harmless sterilisation was only offered to women having their third Caesarian section. I asked permission, which was granted, to offer it to any woman who had had five children naturally, and gradually I reduced that figure to two. Opposition, especially on the grounds of religion, was tremendous at first, but I am proud to say that by the mid-1970s, the birth rate in Liverpool, which had been 30 per cent above the national average, had dropped to slightly below it. Of course that was not all my doing, because abortion was legal by then, and there was increased use of both the contraceptive pill and the coil, but tubal ligation still played a major part.

"I have said I encountered strong opposition, but that is putting it mildly, and some of it came from within my own profession. When Barbara Castle became Minister of Health, she introduced a fee of between £30 and £40 for every sterilisation performed, and the very people who had been my strongest critics changed their attitude almost overnight! I should emphasise that I had never charged for tubal ligation previously".

The strongest opposition, however, came from members of Liverpool's large Roman Catholic population, whose doctrine specifically forbids both abortion and artificial forms of birth control. Mr Francis remembers many dramatic encounters, one of them with an anaesthetist in the middle of an operation. "The lady concerned had had a very difficult pregnancy, and as she already had other children, I asked her if she would like her tubes tied after the delivery. She agreed, but when the baby had been born and I prepared for the ligation, the anaesthetist tore off his mask and gloves, threw them on the floor and walked out on me. Needless to say I was extremely annoyed, because his conduct was not only unprofessional but could have been extremely dangerous". Nor was this an isolated incident. "I was about to tie a woman's tubes on another occasion when a Priest suddenly burst into the ward and called out: 'I call on all present to witness that this woman is about to commit a mortal sin!' The poor woman was terrified, climbed back into bed and told me she had changed her mind. That was bad enough, but not quite as bad as what happened another time, when we were using an overflow bed in the tropical wing of the old Royal Hospital, and a cleaner tipped off the Priest that I was about to tie a woman's tubes there. The Priest came into the ward, went up to the woman and told her he would not be able to give her daughter communion if she agreed to have the operation. Of course she changed her mind.

"I appreciate people have strong feelings on this subject, and of course it is all part of Roman Catholic doctrine, but if you had seen the damage caused by people having too many children, as I have, you would know why I am concerned. I am happy to say the Church seems to be more liberal these days, and they do appear to turn a blind eye far more frequently than they used to. People do not realise that if we did not terminate about 160,000 pregnancies a year in the United Kingdom, the population would be rising to an unbearable level. The birthrate in Eire is much lower than in England, but if you search through the records, you will find that is because their termination rate is much higher. In the past a great many Irish girls used to come to Liverpool on the ferries to have abortions, which didn't feature in any Irish statistics. Catholics often point to Italy, where the birth rate is pretty well static, but they neglect to mention that the legal termination rate there is 50 per cent higher than ours".

Once launched on the subject of birth control and over-population, Mr Francis takes a lot of stopping. The greater his experience, at home and abroad, the greater his conviction that the world is heading for a major crisis unless the one can be effectively applied and the other restricted. "We hear a great deal about so-called Green issues like the threat to world wildlife, the danger to the ozone layer and the pollution of inland waterways, but they are all peripheral to the real problem", he warns. "Every one of these problems, and a great many more, is down to the major issue of there being far too many people. Do you realise, for example, that the world population is growing by about 92 million people, or one and a half times the population of the United Kingdom, each year?

"There are already more than a billion people in China, about 800 million in India and rapidly growing populations all over the African and South American continents. In Kenya, the population is currently doubling every 17 years, and the picture is almost as bad in Brazil, which explains the ruthless destruction of the rain forests to provide food and homes for all the extra people. The consequences are inevitable. There is famine in places like Ethiopia even when they don't suffer from drought, but instead of trying to address the basic problem, all the West does is provide short term aid in the form of food.

"The explosion is partly due to higher standards of health and hygiene, which we all appreciate, but the world simply cannot accommodate all the extra mouths. The additional carbon dioxide that will be emitted by all those additional millions of people in the next 10 years or so is a worse hazard than all the present fumes from vehicles, and don't forget that every man, woman and child is also responsible for a measurable (and considerable) amount of personal sewage. I know that sounds unpleasant, but it is cold hard fact. The more people there are, the more resources they will consume and the more pollution they will generate. It is as simple as that. Since coming to Liverpool I have travelled to many parts of the world, and the same problems exist almost everywhere, although they are obviously worse in some places than others. And they are not helped by the fact that in some undeveloped countries, children are seen as physical assets. In India a child, preferably one that is deformed, helps its parents to beg, or can be sold off for cheap labour in one of those carpet sweat shops. In that situation, you can't be surprised there is opposition to birth control".

Mr Francis' answer has been to involve himself heavily in preaching the gospel by both the written and spoken word. From 1976 to 1983 he was chairman of the Medical Publications Committee of the International Family Planning Federation, the body that links more than 150 family planning associations throughout the world, and he has remained an active member of its advisory board ever since. "Our basic creed is that there must be a direct relationship between the natural resources and productivity of any one area, and the number of people it can support. Obviously that differs from country to country, but as a general guide we believe couples should limit themselves to two children", he says.

"If most people would only do that, the world population would plateau out at the present level. That would still be too high really, because we cannot support the existing population adequately now, but at least it would be a start. If couples average three children, we shall see a rise of 50 per cent, and that is a truly horrific prospect".

Some time ago Mr Francis took a lot of stick for his outspoken critism of Princess Diana, after she had been quoted as saying she would like a large family. "I have no doubt that Prince Charles and her could support more than two, but the fact is that they set an example to a great many other people", says Mr Francis. "If they were to have three or four children, that would soon become the fashion and we would find many families following suit. Prince Charles is extremely vulnerable, because he is now seen as an important spokesman on behalf of the environment. If he were now to become the father of three or four children, he would inevitably lose credibility, because he would then be seen to be consuming more than his fare share of limited natural resources".

Mr Francis has carried out many overseas lecture and teaching tours in undeveloped countries, as one would expect of a man who was invited onto the World Health Organisation's working party on tubal ligation. He has lectured in Malaysia, India and Sri Lanka, and in the seventies inaugurated a scheme for training Iranian doctors at Liverpool Maternity Hospital, which lasted until the start of the Iranian Revolution. He has also paid frequent visits to the Sudan with his wife, helping to treat the President's wife and establishing powerful friendships in that country.

Two heads are better than one. Harold Francis' wife and fellow gynaechologist Winnie Francis, like him a keen supporter of Liverpool F.C., admires one of the club's many trophies.

"I suppose anyone working in Liverpool tends to be internationally-minded", he says. "That is part of the heritage we acquired as one of the world's great seaports. The city was a pioneer in the field of tropical medicine, helping to establish other famous schools abroad, and similarly we have done our best to help the under-developed world in the fields of maternity care and birth control. Unfortunately, you often feel rather helpless because of the size of the problem.

"I have visited Calcutta, one of the world's largest and most congested cities, and believe me it is nothing less than a nightmare. You can go out at night and be unable to find a foot of space to stand on because of all the bodies of people sleeping in the streets. These days it is bad enough in London, where you find famous thoroughfares like the Strand crowded with down-and-outs sleeping rough, but even that does not compare with Calcutta.

"Most people have heard of Mother Theresa, who must be the kindest person in the world. She has devoted her life to helping the destitute of Calcutta and deserves every bit of the praise given her. However, the cruel fact is that her work doesn't get to the root of the basic problem and in fact makes it even worse. She and her staff pick up the sick and the dying, and nurse them back to health, which means there are even more mouths to feed.

"She has been over here three times, and been given a heroine's reception each time. Unfortunately, because she is a Roman Catholic, she is strongly anti-contraception and anti-birth pill. I have said before and I will say it again, Mother Theresa would achieve far more for the good of mankind and womankind, if she were willing to take a shipfull of birth control pills home with her. That would help to ensure a gradual reduction in the teeming millions of Indians who live and die in abject poverty, and have no hope of improving their situation.

"If it is the last thing on earth I do, it is to make sure that my own city of Liverpool never gets like Calcutta. In fact the population of Liverpool, like that of the North West in general, is steadily dropping through economic reasons, and I am extremely thankful. I am sick of hearing the C.B.I. say there is a shortage of school leavers, because there was another wave of births three or four years ago. Don't people ever learn? It is not long since everyone was complaining that unemployment was over three million, and it will remain high so long as the birth rate stays high. Thanks to improved care of the elderly, the annual surplus of births over deaths is about 100,000 and you have to add a regular influx of immigrants onto that".

Some find it strange that a campaigner of such international renown should be based in Liverpool rather than London. Mr Francis makes no apologies. "When I came here originally, I did not expect to stay more than two or three years", he confesses. "All I was seeking was an extension of clinical experience. But time passed, and I have become increasingly involved with the city and its people. And so far as I am concerned, you can enjoy a far higher quality of life in Liverpool than in London. There are some of the most marvellous buildings here, Speke Hall, St. George's Hall, the two great Cathedrals and that magnificent waterfront. Thanks to the far-sightedness of former city fathers, there are also some splendid parks. One of my greatest pleasures is taking my dog for a morning's walk in Sefton Park.

"Winifred and I have been supporters of Liverpool Football Club for many years and often travelled with them into Europe in the days before the Heysel Disaster. They are a superb team, easily the best in the country, and the remarkable thing is that they hardly ever seem to have a poor season. I have made many good friends at Anfield, as well as at other grounds. People sometimes talk as though football is a crude game for the unthinking masses, but that is pure rubbish. We enjoy football, but we also enjoy going to the opera, the theatre and the ballet, and you can do all that in Liverpool as well as anywhere else".

Mr Francis' commitment to his adopted city was such that he even had a brief stab at local politics, representing Aigburth Ward on Liverpool City Council between 1968-72. A staunch Conservative, he was persuaded to stand at a time when that party were gradually losing their influence to the emerging Liberals and the city was suffering from frequent industrial disputes. "So far as I'm concerned Trade and Union are the worst five letter words in the English language", he says. "At that time Liverpool had a dreadful name for poor industrial relations, though I believe things have improved since. Cammell Laird were in the throes of a whole series of demarcation disputes, and that didn't help. I can't say I enjoyed my spell on the Council because it was so frustrating, so I wasn't too worried about being defeated. All three Tories in Aigburth lost our seats to Liberals at the same time. I can remember one of them asking where Aigburth was, shortly before the election, but his ignorance of local geography didn't stop him being returned".

Now semi-retired, Mr Francis has few regrets. "There have been great changes in Liverpool as everywhere else, but thankfully the City has come through them well", he says. "I believe things would have been much worse if we had not done so much to help mothers avoid having children they could not support or did not really want. I firmly believe that sensitive birth control is the only realistic answer to the ever-growing threat of over-population, and I am proud to have made a contribution in the under-developed world as well as in my home city. Hopefully Liverpool will continue the pioneering role for which it is justly famous".

John Hardman

Former Asda chairman John Hardman, who helped to turn a relatively small Yorkshire store company into Britain's third largest retailing group, is very much a son of Liverpool. Born and brought up there alongside several famous contemporaries, he has shared in some of the city's greatest triumphs and suffered through the disasters that transformed its post-war industrial life. Even when he moved to Wetherby to be close to his company headquarters, he remained a member of Royal Liverpool Golf Club, a staunch supporter of Liverpool Football Club and a great believer in the future of what he still thinks of as his home city.

Born in Utting Avenue, before moving slightly up-market to Allerton, John Hardman was educated at Springwood School and Quarry Bank, an establishment that also numbered John Lennon and Oldham manager Joe Royle among its pupils. "It was a fine school, which later became one of the victims of muddle-headed reform", he recalls. "Joe Royle was younger than me, but I remember Lennon well, although we were never very close. He was the original Beatnik, but he didn't really stand out at school, because to do that you had to be good at football or cricket.

"I was fanatically keen on both without being much good, and I was not academic because I couldn't be bothered with classwork. I suppose I was a typical iconoclast, authority was there to be challenged, and heaven knows what would have happened to me but for one of the masters, Sandy Martin. He saved my life. I was doing detention and he came over and gave me a good telling off, talking as man to man and not as master to pupil, which made all the difference. Somehow he made me realise that if I wanted to achieve anything I had to buckle down and work, and I shall always be grateful to him for that.

"Much to everyone's surprise including my own I finished up with quite good 'A' levels and was able to go on to Liverpool University. These days most local kids want to move away when they go to college, but for me there was simply nowhere else because Liverpool was the place to be in the late fifties and the early sixties. It was immensely exciting, what with the rise of the Beatles and the emergence of Bill Shankly's Liverpool. The port still hadn't fully declined, so there was an air of grandeur about the place which you wouldn't find anywhere else. I remember seeing a friend off on the Mauretania and it was a moving sight as she sailed away into the

sunset. I also remember being in San Francisco once and seeing a huge banner that read 'See you in Liverpool'. It was still an incredibly important and glamorous place, and I hope it can be again".

Even in those early days, John Hardman had an inbuilt commercial awareness, probably inherited from his father. "He was a wonderful character", says his proud son. "He was also born in Liverpool, but he virtually brought himself up and left school at 15. He was much brighter than me and extraordinarily resilient, so that if one thing went sour on him he could move straight on to another. He was a cotton broker for a time, then went bust and had to rely on my mother, who ran a small shop. He soon bounced back, joined Vernon's Pools and achieved a certain distinction as the man who invented the Treble Chance. He used to tell me: "Go out and find yourself a job in your spare time. For every pound you make, I'll give you another." That was a marvellous incentive. I got a newspaper round, and did a few other odd jobs, rapidly learning the value of standing on my own feet.

"I hadn't a clue what I wanted to do when I went to university, but Liverpool was a commercial rather than an industrial city, so I took a degree in commerce. Dad suggested I should become a dentist or a doctor or a solicitor. By then he was playing a good deal of golf in mid-week, and there were always plenty of doctors and dentists and solicitors on the course. Dad thought that if they had so much spare time, they must be in the right job!

"However, I wasn't interested in any of those, and eventually I decided to go into accountancy because I reasoned that would at least help me to understand the use of money. I joined Duncan Watson, a splendid old-fashioned firm in Liverpool who had a nice wide range of business, and was articled to Ted Short, who had been the wartime Mayor of Birkenhead. I couldn't have made a better choice as it happened, because it gave me experience that was invaluable for retailing. There is a different ethos in Britain than in the United States or Germany, where most big businesses are run by scientists or engineers. Over here, accountants reign supreme, which is not necessarily a good thing and doesn't say too much for the training given in those other disciplines.

"I was doing quite well, but I didn't fancy staying there for a long time. I had just got married, and with my wife also earning good

Opposite:
Another of Quarry Bank School's famous old boys, along with the late John Lennon. Former Asda superstore chairman and chief executive John Hardman.

money as an air hostess there was no shortage of cash. We were a couple of Yuppies a few years ahead of our time, enjoying ourselves, but not really achieving anything. I was offered a partnership in a small firm, but that seemed to me like a return to the womb and I wasn't ready to be buried. I just had no clear idea what to do next".

The turning point of Hardman's commercial life came when he joined a subsidiary of the Radio Corporation of America (R.C.A.) in Sudbury. Colour television was starting to boom, and R.C.A. decided to build a brand new plant at Skelmersdale New Town, just outside Liverpool, to manufacture colour tubes. The plant was an almost exact replica of the parent company's plant in Pennsylvania, and suddenly Hardman, the company's financial accountant, was plunged straight into the harsh reality of manufacturing on Merseyside.

"It was quite an eye-opener", he says. "Not only did it start my career in electronics, but it forced me to set up my own financial structure from scratch. That was quite new to me, because at that time accountants tended to be mainly concerned with theory and academic bedrock rather than getting to grips with basic issues. Almost overnight I had to learn about recruiting and delegation, and I soon appreciated the importance of finding and keeping good staff.

"I have to say it was a tremendously exciting project at the time, because we were creating something new on a green field site in an area desperate for new forms of employment to compensate for the inevitable decline of a once-great port. That should have been an advantage but it wasn't, because all Liverpool's past had been based on commerce rather than manufacturing and there was no history of well organised and disciplined labour relations. It was a huge plant too, capable of building 1.1 million tubes a year at full capacity, though we never achieved that.

"Initially Thorn Electrics were involved with Radio Rentals, but they bought out of it, and I was left to virtually run the entire place. A lot of staff came from the North East, and although the mixture of Geordies and Scousers had some advantages, it made things difficult in others, because both were used to different working practices. It was a situation typical of many others at the time, with inexperienced management learning as they went, trying to cope with four different unions and a labour force with no tradition of consistently reliable hard work. The workforce were friendly enough, off site, and I even played football with them. I think they regarded me as a sort of management mascot and didn't take me too seriously, but whatever the reason we never achieved anything like the levels of production needed".

An always critical situation grew steadily worse, with mounting competition from cut-price Japanese tubes and a sharp fall in the value of sterling. "The three-day week finished us off", says Hardman sadly. "The company were losing a fortune and there seemed no way of putting matters right. We tried to interest the Labour Government of the time in a rescue operation but they weren't interested, and all our efforts to persuade the Department of Trade and Industry to stop Japanese dumping ended in failure. In those days the balance of payment was in our favour and nobody in authority worried their heads about the Japanese.

"In 1974, the year Liverpool won the F.A. Cup for the second time, we finally closed the factory down. It was a terribly sad time, with a certain unreality about it all. I spent six months selling plant and machinery, and I recall on one occasion even organising a redundancy dance. Typical of Liverpool that, celebrating disaster!

"If I learned one thing more than any other at that time, it was the extent of the North-South divide. Every time we went down to London to plead our case with a Government department, or seek help from other sources, we realised that most of the people who really mattered believed the North was where people made things, and the South was where all the decisions were made. After the factory closed down, people often asked me what had gone wrong. The answer is straightforward enough. It was a mixture of attitude (them and us), ignorance and apathy by a Government who didn't seem to care".

At least John Hardman's employers did not blame him for the factory's closure. He was soon offered a new job back in Pennsylvania, and spent the next six or seven years in a number of different roles, frequently acting as a kind of international trouble-shooter, and learning that for all its strengths, American industry was also far from perfect. "The Americans are far more willing to take risks than we are, and their labour force is used to working hard and meeting tough targets", he explains. "But their companies are riddled with nepotism. One of the first things I was told in New York was to find myself a company guru, that is someone up there at the top who would be willing to keep an eye on me.

"American business is a lot like American politics, which operates in groupings. When your group is in the ascendancy all goes well, but when another group gets control, you just beaver away and keep your head down. I soon found none of the top men at R.C.A. was anything like John Wayne, and when I was moved to New York, the nepotism was unbelievable. If someone up there made a foolish decision, nobody had the courage to object. They just waited for him to be proved wrong and fired. If you told your boss you were wasting money, he would come back and tell you to shut up and not rock the apple cart.

"R.C.A. were headed up by a guy called Ed Griffiths, one of these hard-living, fast-talking executives you often read about who is determined to push profits up every quarter by one means or another. His pet interest was the video disc, and we spent millions developing it, even though everyone else at R.C.A. could see it was time-finished because it had been overtaken by video-tape. Nobody had the balls to tell Ed, even if he would have listened, and so he went on destroying the company. His policy set it back years, and eventually it was taken over by General Electric. We might not have been so hot in Skelmersdale, but after my stint there, I always knew how to recognise failure!"

Most British businessmen who emigrate to the United States end up staying there for good, but not John Hardman. "I suppose the turning point came on my eldest boy's 11th birthday", he muses. "I looked at him and thought, in a few years time he'll have shot off to California and we'll never see each other again. Above all, I didn't want him growing up to be a typical American. Americans are always on the move and nothing seems to be permanent. It's a fine country in many ways, but I suppose I also missed the friendliness and camaraderie I'd grown used to on Merseyside, even if it wasn't all that efficient. I have to say my wife Joan was not nearly as enthusiastic. It can be a wonderful life for women out there — they just lie around in the sunshine all day — and she would have been happy to stay for good. But all credit to her, she backed my decision and didn't try as hard to make me change my mind as most of my American friends. They couldn't understand me at all, because they thought Britain was now very minor League, and they regarded my decision as an act of betrayal".

Returning to Britain was a traumatic experience, as one might expect. John Hardman came back to Merseyside, where R.C.A. owned a small company, Oriel Foods, and found the place much changed. Apart from the weather, as wet and gloomy as ever, he encountered dirt and dereliction and apathy that made him wonder if he had made the right decision. "Having stood back for a time, one could see a lot of difference, and not everything had improved", he admits. "The town seemed very drab after the nice green suburbs of most American towns, and it took me a couple of years to settle down at Prenton, But it's surprising how quickly time passed, and after a couple of years I found myself thinking of America as just one of those experiences.

"Actually I didn't stay with Oriel Foods very long, because R.C.A. sold the company. We tried to organise what would have been one of the first management buy-outs in this country, but in the end Sir James Gulliver bought it for his Argyll Foods Group. I stayed on a little longer, but by then I had met some of the Asda people and realised there was a much better chance of making my mark with them. I still didn't know exactly where I wanted to go, but it was obvious that Asda offered an excellent opportunity, because they were a relatively small company whose management team were all getting on a bit and looking for new blood. I joined them as finance director, became managing director in 1984, and was eventually chosen to be chairman four years later".

John Hardman's move could hardly have come at a more challenging time. He freely admits the job was the hardest he had ever faced in his life, as his company fought against mounting competition during a period of constant change. "We had just 60 stores when I joined, and well over 200 when I left" he points out.

"Asda was a wonderful company then, but it was falling behind its competitors. And this was happening at the very time when the retailing scene was changing dramatically in terms of both content and scale. In the past, the big retail groups tended to concentrate on a particular area, with Asda mainly in Yorkshire, but then the big five (Sainsbury, Tesco, Asda, Co-op and Safeway) started to establish themselves nationally competing on a national scale. When I arrived, we were already trailing behind, and it meant a great deal of sweat and hard work and investment to catch up.

"So far as content is concerned, we had to appreciate that the consumer is becoming more affluent (even on Merseyside) more health conscious and much more choosy. There is now a growing emphasis on fresh, healthy food and on convenience food, because these days a far larger proportion of all women go to work. That in turn has meant spending a great deal of time and money on design, because food is only part of our content, And you can't put clothes and butter side by side. As you know, we took a major step forward on the clothes side, by coming to an agreement with George Davis, the original creator of Next, for him to sell his designs in some of our stores. For the first time, housewives could buy quality fashion and high class food in the same place.

"Of course all this meant more and more investment. We spent a fortune on things like product development, involving creation of our own brands, and stock control, which in turn involved the use of modern technology. Personally I found this the most interesting side of the business, because it was always changing and always offering

Nice to be back home. John Hardman and his Liverpool born associate George Davis, founder of Next, celebrate the opening of a new Asda store in Liverpool.

new opportunities. My only regret was that life became so busy and so complicated that it was increasingly difficult to keep up with what was going on. I feel I should read a lot more than I do, but it is a matter of finding the time. One thing is for sure, I couldn't do a straightforward audit, as I was originally trained to do, these days because I haven't been involved in that kind of exercise for years."

Sadly, things went sour for both John Hardman and Asda in early 1991, when high interest rates and the start of the recession combined to cripple a company which had been forced to borrow heavily in order to fund rapid expansion. In particular, the purchase of the Gateway stores proved prohibitively expensive, plunging Asda heavily into debt and forcing a change of direction.

John Hardman left the company by mutual agreement with his task still not completed, and has since had to watch in frustration as others seek to bring his dream of making Asda one of Britain's finest retail giants, to fruition.

One thing that has given John Hardman considerable pleasure is the presence of 10 Asda stores in his homeland of Merseyside. That represented a major change of direction after he took over, and has, he says, been fully justified by results. "The company tended to avoid the area at one time, probably because of its unfortunate image", he agrees. "We did open one at Huyton in the early days, but our next one in Kirkby had to close and we stayed away for some time. When we started to look at Hunts Cross, many people were surprised, until they discovered what a good area it was. Both the Hunts Cross and Aintree stores became among our most successful.

"Of course I am a lot more experienced these days than I was in the Thorn days at Skelmersdale, and I think I know a lot more about handling people. That is invaluable, especially on Merseyside, where you have to get the workforce on your side if you are going to achieve any kind of success. It's typical of the place that they view outsiders of any kind with suspicion, and all too often that means management. In the old days it was a bit like travelling on a pre-war train. You had first class, second class and third class citizens who were all supposed to know their place.

"Much of the trouble has been caused by the drastic economic changes that followed the decline of the port, which had given Liverpool the reason for its existence. Both national and local government probably did their best, but it was all piecemeal. There was no game plan from within the city, setting out clear cut objectives for the future. Certainly there were plans, and some of them were highly ambitious, but invariably they were put forward by professional planners who had not consulted the people directly involved. One after the other they had to be abandoned in midstream, with the result that the ordinary man in the street became rather cynical. You can still see the half finished pedestrian walkways in places like Old Hall Street, which had to be abandoned. And again it was typical of Liverpool policy, that when it came to clearing up after the war, thousands of people were moved out, leaving large areas of wasteland that soon became a target for vandals".

John Hardman believes economic decline has inevitably had its effect on the people, who will need time (and hopefully a taste of greater prosperity) to fully recover. "I noticed the difference immediately I returned after 15 years away", he says. "People have become more introverted, and there is a hard edge to the place now. Even the humour for which Liverpool is famous has gone a bit sour. It's still funny, but the jokes tend to be a little on the cruel side. People have started to look inwards, so that the old them-and-us attitude has started to apply to Liverpudlians and those living elsewhere, instead of just management and workers. You hear a lot of wingeing. Nothing is ever Liverpool's fault, it's always supposed to be the fault of someone else, the Government, the Ministry, the D.H.S.S. or whatever.

"That may sound a little harsh but I believe it's true, and the only way it can be stopped is for those of us who have been comparatively successful, to try and put something back. Far too many have simply moved away and left Liverpool to look after itself. Just as some of the wealthy shipowners and cotton brokers moved out to Wirral in the past, so nowadays a great many managers with national companies move in, do as short a stint as possible without involving themselves more than they have to, and move on to higher things.

"The city also needs a better lead from the Council. That has been dominated by people who seem to believe they can develop policies by themselves, outside the real world of hard competition. The Council must not be afraid of business, because that is the lifeblood that provides money and employment for everyone. There is an urgent need for business, Council and ordinary people to come together and support achievable objectives, instead of wasting

"Come right in. We've got everything you want." Hardman opens his arms in *welcome at the opening of another Liverpool Asda store.*

energy and money fighting each other. If anyone doubts whether that can be done, he should look at the example of Glasgow. That was in a worse state than Liverpool not so very long ago, yet now it is booming with every hope for the future. Public relations is vital, and I don't mean the carefully vetted issue of propaganda. Public relations is something that is the responsibility of every single person. The street cleaner or the shopper who takes trouble to answer an inquiry politely is just as important an ambassador as the Lord Mayor".

John Hardman is entitled to his comments because he has put his money where his mouth is. Not only did he bring Asda stores to Merseyside in defiance of popular opinion and support local causes like Alder Hey Children's Hospital and the Mersey Marathon, he also included a strong Merseyside contingent among his top management. His chief executive was another Liverpudlian, trained by the Littlewoods Group, and so was the man he brought in to revamp Asda's fashions, George Davis. "Clothing was an area that had been letting us down", he explains. "We were too down-market and we needed something to give us a boost.

"Quality has to be top priority these days, and I am not ashamed to admit we modelled ourselves on Marks and Spencer in many ways. People sometimes complain they are expensive, but look at their reputation, their turnover and their profits. Our aim was to offer Marks and Spencer quality at lower prices, and we believed we could do that because we operated in out of town areas rather than city centres, making our costs much lower.

"I think there could be a lesson there for Liverpool. I believe the city still has immense potential if it can only get its act together. And to do that, the various elements must come together in partnership, help each other, and try to set higher standards in every way from cleanliness to service. No city has produced so many outstanding individuals, or presents such a major challenge".

Carla Lane

Liverpool has always been a city of great eccentrics, and they don't come much more eccentric than Carla Lane. The girl who left school without so much as a single 'O'-level pass and married a naval architect when only 17, went on to become one of television's best-known script-writers, with half-a-dozen household favourites like "The Liver Birds", "Butterflies" and "Bread" to her credit, devoting much of the proceeds to her lifetime passion, animal rights.

Born Romana Barrach, and brought up in West Derby's Russian Drive, she comes from a long line of seafarers, which helps to explain her enduring fascination for the docks. "They were always a place of nostalgia and excitement", she recalls. "There was movement and bustle everywhere. It was like a little world of its own. I loved the trains that used to chug in and out through the dock gates, and I was fascinated by the huge towers and walls that cut the docks off from everywhere else. They were like mediaeval fortifications.

"All the male members of my family had been to sea. My father was a chief engineer in the Merchant Navy and my grandfather had been head chef on the 'Britannic'. My brother was another chief engineer with Blue Funnel, who had 50 or 60 ships based here at one time, and I ended up marrying a naval architect, so I have always had salt water in my blood. There is nothing like a great seaport, because it is so alive and cosmopolitan. The port of Liverpool may have declined in size, but its history is part of our heritage and it affects the way we think and behave".

Carla freely admits she was no scholar at school. "I disliked it very much", she says. "I went to West Derby Village School, and I generally finished up 32nd in a class of 34. The only subject I was any good at was English, and I did manage to win a prize for some poetry I wrote once. I always enjoyed poetry, and when the children were young, in later years, and things started to get on top of me, I used to relax by slipping out into the garden and writing verse in the summerhouse. To be honest I don't remember too much about my schooldays. There was a Miss Pickworth who used to spit through a hole between her front teeth whenever she spoke (we all competed to avoid the front row!) and a Miss Price, who was very strict. Otherwise, nobody left an enduring impression".

On leaving school, Carla Lane took a job in a small shop selling baby linen, then moved to Henderson's, a large department store in the city centre which was later destroyed by fire. However she was only 17 when she met and married Arthur Hollins, soon giving up her job to bring up her two sons Carl and Nigel, and look after the first of a long line of domestic pets. "I have always had a feel for birds and animals, and it has now become the major passion of my life", she says. "When I was a child I loved almost everything about Liverpool, whether it was the parks or the fine buildings like St. George's Hall or even the rows of terraced houses, but there was always one obscene black blot on the landscape. Stanley Abattoir. I used to watch the trucks full of lambs and calves and pigs go past, and see their outline through the wooden slats and listen to the sound they made, and I used to feel sick.

"That was when I first began to care about animals, and I made up my mind I must try to do something about it, though I didn't actually become a vegetarian until I was in my mid-thirties. I have never tried to tell other people what they should do or what they should think, but it does upset me that people seem to take the misuse of animals for granted. I believe they should care about how slices of meat arrive on their plates, and they should be concerned that the animals are made to suffer as little as possible.

"There wasn't a great deal I could do about it when I was a child or even when I was first married, but now that I am independent and lucky enough to be earning good money, I do what I can to help. I have started a trust called Animal Line, and we collect money for the rescue of creatures which have been hurt or abandoned by their owners, with the long-term hope of buying a stretch of woodland for an animal sanctuary. I am also a patron of the Freshfield Animal Rescue service run by a wonderful lady from Liverpool called Lesley Tarleton. Everything seems to be against her, but she manages to keep cheerful and does wonderful work. I think she is symbolic of what Liverpool people can do when they feel strongly about something. The harder the task and the tougher the opposition, the better they perform".

"I have been extremely lucky to land on my feet and put myself in a position where I am relatively well paid, and so able to indulge my love for animals. In fact these days, they come even before my writing. If I am ever remembered for anything in future years, I hope it will be for my work on their behalf. I don't suppose my enthusiasm has rubbed off on too many other people, but if I have one dream above all others, it is that one day my lovely city of Liverpool will make a significant gesture towards animal welfare. What kind of gesture? Well perhaps everyone could agree to give up meat for a day. That would make a tremendous impression".

*Just one of the family. Carla Lane
with one of the dogs who have played
such a major part in her life.*

Carla Lane's involvement continues to be direct and every day. It
is many years since she had less than a couple of dogs and a cat or two
to look after at home, and at the time of writing she boasts a
miniature menagerie at the large house in Chiswick which she shares
with her sister and brother-in-law. That includes three dogs, seven
cats, two rabbits, two guinea pigs, two tortoises, a number of fish —
both in bowls and a pond outside, three parrots, 72 other birds of
other descriptions — all flying free, and an unspecified number of
pigeons.

"Obviously we have to keep some of them carefully segregated or
the numbers might start to fall", she points out, "but in general they

get on with each other very well. I live by the river, and the cats love to wander outside and sit on the bank. I suppose I spoil them, because they all have their own hand-painted dishes, but they deserve it because they are so intelligent. If I put a dish in the wrong place, the cat concerned will not eat from it, and just waits until I have moved it back again. When it is feeding time, I ring a little handbell, and they all troop out from wherever they are and sit down like so many human beings round a dinner table.

"We have taken in all sorts of creatures over the years, but I must emphasise that it isn't true we go out into the streets searching for ones to rescue. I suppose if you find an injured bird, take it in and feed it, it is only logical that it will tend to stay with you instead of flying off and having to look after itself again. I suppose some people will say I am soft or ridiculous, but I don't mind if they do. I believe animals and birds and fish all have their own place on earth, just like we do, and that they are also entitled to a little consideration".

Carla Lane's family of animals is possibly some kind of compensation for the human family she gradually lost with the development of her writing career and the breakdown of her marriage. It is a matter of history, which she rarely discusses, that once her sons had grown up, Carla set out for London with her friend Myra Taylor and embarked on a writing career which was immediately and spectacularly successful. Without past experience of any kind she submitted scripts to the B.B.C. and, unlike the vast majority of similar adventurers, received a favourable response. Suddenly, she was writing the script for 'Bless This House', the popular comedy series starring Syd James, and being asked for more and more work. When she then wrote 'The Liver Birds', a series about a couple of young Liverpool girls living away from home, she had established herself as a front-line writer, and created a brand new and highly successful career.

"It's a love, a kind of compulsion", she said at the time. "It's my personal fulfilment and escapism. I don't much enjoy suburbia and domesticity. When I am writing, I can detach myself completely and move into another world where I can decide what happens. Writing is something I decided I would have a go at, and now I am trapped. I sometimes tell myself to give it up while there is still time, but I can't. It is as if I have become an addict, and am left with very little choice in the matter".

At first, Carla Lane lived extremely frugally in "a squalid little Paddington bed-sit" for four months of the year, returning to the big family home in West Derby at regular intervals. However, her new career attracted her more and more frequently to where it was all happening, even though she admitted that was causing her to live a horribly lonely existence. Eventually, and most will believe inevitably, her marriage broke up, and she moved to London virtually full time, although paying frequent visits to Merseyside to keep in touch with other members of her family. Indeed, the belief in 'Family' which is brought out so strongly in her 'hit' series 'Bread' seems to have permeated the whole of her life. 'Claremont' in West Derby was always shared by mother and sister and brothers, even her husband stayed on for some years after the divorce, and today it remains in the ownership of a son.

"Anyone who comes from Liverpool knows the importance of that family feeling", Carla says with obvious conviction. "It is that sort of place, very, very clannish and close knit and compassionate, and full of genuine warmth. For me Liverpool is a special place. I know a lot of people say that and many of them don't really mean it, but it is certainly special to me. Perhaps it is not so obvious in the city centre or among the big houses in the suburbs, but just walk down some of the side streets, among the little terraced or semi-detached houses, and you can almost feel the atmosphere.

"I have written several series for televison, and most of them don't really have very much to do with Liverpool. Even in Liver Birds, the two young girls were typical of many elsewhere. But 'Bread' was different. So far as I am concerned that is Liverpool, and the attitudes and atmosphere are those of my home city. I am sure there will be those who criticise, either because they don't like the image I have tried to create, or because they don't think it is accurate, but I honestly think it is a fair portrait.

"The emphasis on family probably has something to do with the large number of immigrants who used to arrive from Ireland. They arrived in families and they had to stick together to survive in what was undoubtedly a tough environment. That probably rubbed off on other members of the community too. The dockers were always very influential and seemed to be involved in a non-stop war with the employers, so they also appreciated the value of sticking together. It has been a fact of life in Liverpool for longer than I can remember, that you are either with them or against them.

"If there is one thing that symbolises Liverpool for me, it is the number of little old Mams, there used to be. Many used to work on the market, and I can still see their pink, scrubbed faces, their black shawls and the little cross-shaped earings they used to wear. I can still hear them shouting 'Luvly white celery!' and exchanging jokes with each other. For me, the Mams of Liverpool were the salt of the earth and I still have great faith in them. I'm not ashamed to say that My Mam is still the Queen of Queens to me".

The image of Liverpool portrayed in 'Bread' by Carla Lane is not entirely flattering. Most of the Boswell family are on the make, and none of them appears to hold down a regular job for any length of time. "I hope they represent what I think of as the endearing skull-duggery of Liverpool's people", she says. "I love that, and it was intended to be the theme of 'Bread'. The image of the city comes over as I have always seen it, it's a truthful image of a place with a great deal to commend it. I wasn't trying to write a series about industrial development or economic progress. 'Bread' is a social commentary on a group of people and their relationships.

"I think Nellie Boswell, for example, comes over as a typical Liverpool Mam, always concerned about the rest of the family and ready to do virtually anything for them. And however badly the other members of the family may behave from time to time, they are always quick to rally round and help in an emergency. Now that really is typical of Liverpool and its people. If you fall down, there is always someone around to pick you up and give a helping hand. What's more, they don't wait to ask who you are and if you have any money, and did you deserve to be in trouble. They just get stuck in and help out without any questions.

"That attitude helped a great deal during the war, when Liverpool took a terrible hammering from the German bombers. When whole roads are wiped out and rows of houses destroyed, everyone has to pitch in and help each other. Times have changed, but not the attitude of the Liverpool people. So many of them are used to having very little, that they are prepared to assist those with even less. It is a fact of life, which is demonstrated whenever people hold collections for charity, that you find the most generosity among those who have the least to give.

"I don't think things can have changed too much, because the whole nation saw what happened after the Hillsborough Disaster. Where else, would an entire city have rallied round to help the bereaved, to try and comfort them and give them every kind of assistance possible? There was a remarkable feeling of togetherness, with thousands of people who didn't even know each other previously, behaving just like the members of one vast family. And as you would have noticed, their grief is unashamed. Liverpool people are full of emotion, and they show their feelings openly. I remember seeing someone describing the death of his daughter, only the other day, and it was really poetic. It came over almost like a soliloquy".

Without being slapstick comedy, Carla Lane's series have invariably been extremely humorous, as one might expect from the daughter of a city known for its comedians. However, she is adamant that the real Liverpool humour is unconscious, dead-pan and virtually spontaneous. "Just listen to any group of people in a pub or shop and you can't help being amused", she points out. "The comments are dry, under-stated and all the funnier for being so closely related to real life. The best and most memorable remarks I have heard, have almost all come out perfectly naturally. It used to be said that you had to have a sense of humour to survive in Liverpool, and although I think that is rather cruel, there is no doubt that an ability to see the ridiculous side of things must help to overcome adversity.

"I often miss that native Liverpool wit when I am away in London, because it is very special to the city. In a way it is typical of the bouncy, brash attitude of the best young people,who can give as much as they take and are always ready for a good-natured argument. I noticed it particularly among the young girls, whom I think are the best and brightest in the country. I love Liverpool girls because they are so smart, so bouncy and so pretty. It is as though they are on wires, they bounce so much, and they never seem to be depressed, or even at a loss for words for very long.

"Rather surprisingly, in view of Liverpool's economic decline, there always seems to be plenty of optimism about. It is very hard to get a true Liverpudlian down, because he invariably sees the funny side of things and is ready to bounce up again and set off in a different direction. In fact there is almost a feeling of arrogance at times, not an unpleasant one, but just an expression of self-confidence or cockiness, which is sometimes misunderstood by people elsewhere. I have always felt at home in Liverpool, and even though I now live in the London area, I still love to come back from time to time, wander round the city, and look up my old friends. Once a Liverpudlian, you are always a Liverpudlian".

A total realist, Carla admits there are a few things about Liverpool that she doesn't like. "I dislike a great many of the more recent buildings in and around the city very much indeed", she says. "They lack character, and I think that is sad when you look at some of the wonderful buildings put up in the past. We have a wonderful waterfront, and I can't fault what is being done to reclaim the docks, but so many buildings in the city centre are the worst kind of eyesores. They look just like those awful ante-natal clinics. I miss the old churches which have been pulled down, and I also miss some of those lovely little back cracks in the city centre, with funny little shops and pubs in them. I suppose that is part of the price we have to pay for progress.

All good friends and vegetarians together. Carla Lane (centre) with her close friends Linda and Paul McCartney.

"The other thing I dislike is something that has only crept in comparatively recently, and that is the jealousy, you could almost say hatred, of success. You find cars vandalised just because they are new and shiny, or flowers pulled up because a garden looks pretty. I have seen slogans like "Kill the rich" sprayed on motorway flyovers or the walls in public spaces, and I find that depressing. They have always been plenty of poor people in Liverpool, as in any other big city, but there used not to be this feeling of bitter resentment. It is an unfortunate sign of the times, and I believe it does harm to the very people who spray the slogans.

"If Liverpool is to become prosperous again, as we all hope, it will only be through the unified efforts of a lot of people. How can potential employers be expected to go there if they encounter that kind of bitterness when they come to have a look round? What's more, it is terribly damaging to the image of Liverpool outside, and that is already bad enough. The warmth and friendliness of our people should really be a huge asset, as is our sense of humour, and it would be a great shame if the effect of that was spoiled by a group of malcontents. Liverpool may have had to suffer more than its fare share of injustice in recent years, but that is nothing new, and in the past it managed to face even worse problems with dignity".

Carla freely acknowleges her debt to her Liverpool background and upbringing. "I base my writing on what I observe around me, and on what I feel", she explains. "I have always had a lively imagination, and it is common for me to look at someone, find their appearance intriguing, and start creating the most vivid pictures of what I think they are really like, in my mind. I was like that even as a small child, and would sit for hours making up little stories about quite ordinary people I had seen or met, imagining them doing all sorts of exciting things.

"I rarely model one of my characters on an actual person, but I suppose they all bear substantial traces of real people I have come across at one time or another. Take Nellie Boswell. She wasn't modelled on any particular person, but is representative of hundreds of those lovely Liverpool Mams I mentioned previously.

"It is quite a responsibility, because if people see 'Bread' as typifying the City of Liverpool I have to make sure that picture is accurate and fair. I have worked for the B.B.C. for quite a long time now, and I am trusted to produce a truthful image, which will not give a distorted picture. Obviously the story lines are all fiction, but the background and environment against which they take place have to be clearly authentic.

"Joey and the others may be seen as scallywags, who live on their wits, but don't forget that is true of life in any big city. Liverpool is a brave place and it is full of humour, but it is also a jungle, whose inhabitants have to survive in a particular situation. It wouldn't help anyone to pretend otherwise. But for all its faults and all its problems, it will always remain my spiritual home".

Alfie Lewis

So far as the outside world is concerned, Liverpool is full of stereotypes, comedians, footballers, Council 'skivers', striking dockers and television playwrights. In particular, the district of Toxteth has its own distinctive public image since the infamous riots, so it may surprise many to know that one of its most dangerous-looking inhabitants is nothing less than a modern crusader. Twenty-nine-year-old Alfie Lewis may be the reigning world heavyweight kick-boxing champion, a karate international and a man capable of striking fear into the bravest heart, but he is also a softie who loves children, and a businessman who has shown himself willing to commit time and money to the rehabilitation of his native city.

"I was born in Toxteth, I live there now and I intend to go on doing just that", he says with quiet conviction. "I believe in Liverpool and its people, who have had a lousy time for many years, and I want to do what I can to make things better. Thankfully, I think the tide has begun to turn, and I want to be here when it reaches the shore. Far too many successful people have made their reputation here and then left. I have done well enough to make a living somewhere else, but I am determined to stay and try to help the many others who have been a lot less fortunate".

Alfie Lewis has been fighting, in one way or another, throughout his life. "No, I can't say I was bullied at school, because I was bigger than most of the other kids, so if anything it was me they were afraid of", he admits with a reluctant grin. "I started boxing when I was seven, and a guy called Billy Macks used to have me out every morning running round the park. I kept that up for quite a long time and even made the regional squad, but I disliked being hit in the face and decided I would rather concentrate on something that wasn't quite so painful. It may sound strange, but for me martial arts have always been a form of sport, not a form of war. I don't see any point in deliberately setting out to try and hurt other people, or to be hurt by them, and believe me, there is no way I would let my children run the risk of serious injury. Pain is a part and parcel of most forms of competition, but you have to keep it within reason and I am totally opposed to hurting people for the sake of it".

As well as boxing, the young Lewis also excelled at basketball, judo, athletics — "I was quite a nippy sprinter" — and rather surprisingly fencing. He was, in fact, like many young Liverpudlians, a highly competent all-round sportsman, though not particularly fond of soccer, the area's number one sporting pastime. "I didn't achieve a great deal at school, probably because I was too busy doing other things", he admits, "but I think I must have been a bit of an academic at heart, because later on I took O-Levels in maths, geography, history and home economics at night school. I have always liked reading, and books have helped me enormously by introducing me to the theory behind so many sports.

"One of my favourite books, which I still read regularly, is the Japanese Tsun-Su book, which is virtually a guide to the art of war, and is required reading for many Japanese businessmen. It makes you understand the thinking behind so many tactical manoeuvres, and teaches you the value of total concentration. That is something most top sportsmen work at very hard, though sometimes what they do is not properly appreciated by the public. A perfect example was the tennis ace Bjorn Borg, who concentrated so hard on court that he didn't appear to be interested and was always being criticised for his failure to show emotion.

"I have worked at this so hard that on a couple of occasions in my kick-boxing career I have suddenly found myself looking down on myself as a spectator! It may sound a bit weird, but it's perfectly true. I could see my opponent and myself quite objectively, analyse what I was doing, and work out a plan for victory. Of course it all happened a great deal more quickly than that suggests, so far as combat was concerned, with all my faculties perfectly attuned and everything in total harmony. When you reach that state, your reactions become automatic, in that you are so keyed up and so well prepared that you react to an opponent's move without really thinking". With such a mental approach, it is perhaps hardly surprising that one of Lewis' favourite relaxations is chess! "My wife Donna is very intelligent, and I enjoy playing her", he says. "I used to stay behind at school to learn the rudiments, and I only wish I knew a little more about it. Luckily I have a computer at home, and I enjoy playing against that, though I suppose it's not quite like taking on a Master".

As a competitor, Lewis has long been one of the best British champions, if one of the least publicised. He has held a world title for four years, moving up a weight to take the heavyweight crown in 1991, though he had a narrow escape in the semi-final. "The event is a semi-contact sport, but I caught my opponent with a kick that broke his jaw", he explains reluctantly. "Quite apart from concern about him, I thought I might be disqualified, but luckily the jury decided that he was to blame for the injury, rather than me, because he had made an incorrect response. Kick-boxing and karate have a lot in common, and I compete at karate on the international circuit too, but it is kick-boxing which is really my speciality. The trouble with

*Violence under strict control. Alfie
Lewis demonstrates part of his
technique to guests at the opening of
his Martial Arts Centre.*

karate is that there are several different styles and at least two ruling bodies, so it is hard to say who is really the best. That's why it has still not been accepted as an Olympic sport.

"I think it is a pity that neither karate nor kick-boxing enjoy the sort of publicity that is given to boxing, because they require far more skill and are followed by far more people. Yet while some very ordinary boxers become national heroes and earn large sums of money, I could mention many martial arts champions who are almost totally unknown outside their sport. I have always been strongly aware of this, because I was born on the same day as Frank Bruno, who has made such a name for himself and must be close to being a millionaire. I have nothing against Frank, who seems a perfectly nice character, but as a top sportsman he's a joke. I would be only too delighted to take him on any time, on a winner-take-all basis, but I can't ever see him agreeing to that! As a heavyweight, I fight opponents of up to 17 stone, although I am only just over 14 stone myself, so Frank's greater size would not worry me — and anyway I doubt if he would ever land a punch".

Quite apart from his fighting skills, Alfie Lewis is an enthusiastic teacher and instructor. "I've always been able to communicate with other people", he says. "When I was still a teenager I had a lot to do with a guy called George Willington, who used to buy up derelict buildings and open them up as sports centres, with the accent on martial arts. He used to set everything up, and then leave me to run them even though I was only 16 at the time. I worked in Stockport, Manchester and Sheffield among other places, and found it easy to get on with the kids, even though I had never had any formal training. I can't explain why, but I seem to have some kind of rapport with children. There have been times in Toxteth when schools have rung me up and asked me to have a word with a troublesome kid rather than contacting his parents". In later years, Lewis has become increasingly involved with the City Council. With his size, background and influence in the local community, especially among coloured people, he was an obvious choice for security work at big events like pop concerts, and he was also employed for a time as one of Councillor Derek Hatton's Minders. Eventually he became one of the city's sports development officers in a Leisure Department which has contributed more than most to the quality of life within the Inner City, and gradually began to think about the possibility of organising some kind of sports and community centre himself.

"I thought it was important that someone from within Toxteth should run a centre in Toxteth, so that he would have the trust and support of the local people, which is very hard for an outsider", says

Lewis. "There is a very long history of suspicion which takes a great deal to overcome. It isn't really a racial thing, though it may help me that I am coloured, more the fact that the area as a whole has been deprived and messed around for a long time, often by people who have very little general interest in it.

"Martial arts has an advantage in that it is comparatively uncomplicated and quite cheap. You don't have to have elaborate equipment or an artificial pitch, and of course there is no denying that activities seen to be physically demanding tend to be very attractive. I thought that if we could establish a centre of excellence, it would not only help to keep kids off the street, but could be used to teach them good manners and habits which would be good for the entire community. I am a great believer in self-discipline and unfortunately that isn't something that is always taught in the home these days. If young people can be encouraged to show consideration for other people, exercise proper self-control and take a pride in what they are doing, that can only benefit the quality of life in Toxteth".

Lewis' dream must have sounded an unlikely one when he first mentioned it, but fortunately his words fell on receptive ears. The Toxteth Task Force, set up in the wake of the riots, were especially supportive, the City Council were happy to support one of their own men, and the regional Sports Council soon realised this was an initiative to be applauded. Contact was made with Whitbread's Brewery, who carried out a thorough investigation and then promised additional finance, preparing the way for one of the most imaginative developments seen in Liverpool or any other troubled city.

An old tumbledown building was acquired in Solway Street, just off Lodge Lane in the heart of Toxteth, and on June 26 1991, the new, privately-controlled Centre of Excellence was declared officially open. Ironically, the ceremony was not performed by the person originally chosen by Lewis as the perfect role model for Toxteth youth. Due to an administrative mix-up, former Liverpool soccer giant Kenny Dalglish failed to arrive, though one felt he would have approved the principles behind the project. "So far as I am concerned, Kenny Dalglish is the epitome of what a true sportsman should be", Lewis insists. "He has always been a true professional, who dedicates himself to trying to achieve perfection, and you have never found him cutting training, misbehaving in public, or attempting to cheat. Lots of sporting stars can be seen fooling about in night-clubs or playing around with women, but Dalglish has always been the sportsman's sportsman".

*Action man. Alfie Lewis gets a kick
out of training.*

Although only a comparatively small club at the moment, Lewis
could report 180 members within the first fortnight, with morning
and evening classes in a wide range of activities, fully-booked well in
advance. In addition to akai-jitsu, ju-jitsu, karate, judo and kick-
boxing, it offers instruction in weight-training, fencing and aerobics
for women as well as men and in particular for children. "I'm afraid
that by the time a person has reached his or her early twenties, he
tends to be set in his ways", Lewis explains. "In the long run, our
number one priority has to be with the kids, because we can teach
them good habits right from the start. At the moment they are falling
over each other to join. Our youngest recruit is just three years old,
and we have half-a-dozen who are six or younger".

Significantly, Lewis' club caters strictly for members only. "We have to have total control from the start, and the last thing I want is for a couple of cowboys to come in off the street and start messing around", he points out. "We ask people to apply, check them out and then bring them in as you would at a golf or tennis club. We charge an annual subscription of £30, and then people pay £1.50 per session before 4.00 pm and £2.00 afterwards. We are not offering free admission for the unemployed, because many of them have as much cash as you or me. My experience is that people will always pay for anything they value and we want them to value membership".

Rather surprisingly, the club is now run as a private venture. Although initially funded by public money and help from the brewery, Lewis operates it as a commercial business, rather as a leisure company would run a tennis or health club in prosperous Guildford. The building may be a little down-market, with a rubble-strewn car park round the corner from a street littered with rubbish, but the basic principle behind it all is one of free enterprise, hardly something one expects to find in the middle of Toxteth.

Lewis is unrepentant. "There is nothing at all wrong with business, provided that business has a heart and takes account of the needs of the community", he emphasises. "People have always been willing to pay a reasonable price for the things they need, and there are few things that Toxteth people need more than the chance to work hard, keep fit and maintain their self-respect. I have not met anyone who complains about our charges, and I think it is only reasonable that my instructors and I should be able to make a fair living. The local authority and the Task Force have helped us to start; now it is up to us to demonstrate that we can make a go of the whole thing.

'Our aim is to achieve excellence, and to that end we have brought in people from outside Toxteth to help us achieve it. Some of the instructors and members here come from quite a distance, although the majority are obviously based in this neighbourhood. They all have something to contribute, and there is no question of them taking up places needed by local people. Obviously we don't have enough first class instructors in all the various disciplines right on our own doorstep. As an approved centre of excellence, we hope to attract outstanding performers from quite a wide area, just as the city gymnastics centre in Steble Street does and just as Liverpool and Everton do in football.

"Because of its situation, I expect the hard core of our members will always be from Toxteth, but if we include outstanding individuals from elsewhere it can only be good for everyone. Some people have asked whether one of our aims is to help the coloured community enjoy greater opportunities, but really the centre has nothing to do with colour, any more than it has to do with race or religion. There are people of all kinds and all colours and all nationalities round here, as there always have been in Liverpool, and generally speaking they get on very well. However, it must help communal spirit if they are able to compete and enjoy themselves in a disciplined and well-organised environment".

Discipline is a key word, as it always is in martial arts, where inattention to rules and proper behaviour can prove extremely dangerous. Students of judo, ju-jitsu and karate invariably start a session by saluting each other, and there is an impressive atmosphere of self-respect and dignity, with the instructor or contest official completely in command. Even so, it comes as something of a shock to see that Lewis' club has devised its own "Code of Life" which members agree to obey to the letter, which is displayed prominently on the gymnasium wall, and which is repeated out loud before and after every children's training session.

It reads as follows:—

We shall always strive to better our world for the benefit of everyone;
We shall always protect the old, the weak and the innocent;
We shall always seek to improve the way we live;
We shall never accept the wrongdoing of others;
We shall always give respect regardless of race, age, colour, or creed;
We shall never pre-empt an attack, and only use our skills in self-defence;
We shall always honour our word.
THIS I SWEAR.

"As I said before, one of our main objectives here is to improve and develop standards of behaviour", Lewis points out. "That is almost more important than providing opportunities for competition. I have lived in Toxteth and Liverpool all my life, and there are many fine people here, but we all know there are some others, who behave badly and can cause trouble for everyone. In many cases, that is largely due to the way they have been brought up, and to their lack of opportunities. Obviously it is not easy to make an impression on them, but if we can get to the children and the sports-minded, and through them to their parents, I believe we can achieve a great deal.

"I have never had any problems walking through Toxteth on my own, even at night, largely because I can look after myself and because I am well-known, but it saddens me that a lot of women and older people do not feel safe going out after dark. That is a shame and should not happen in a great city. It is only a few who cause the problems, and we must all campaign to discourage them, and to encourage the vast majority to take actual pleasure in behaving themselves".

All the indications are that Alfie Lewis' initiative will be successful, because there is immense enthusiasm for martial arts on Merseyside. The City has produced a world judo champion in Ann Hughes and a large number of British and European karate champions, although most of them embrace a different code from that followed by Lewis. "There are a great many people interested in martial arts, but mainly as competitors rather than spectators", Lewis points out. "At major competitions, you will find the audience is extremely knowledgable, because so many of them are participants, but unfortunately the sport is not so popular with the general public because it tends to be rather technical. Most people can follow a boxing match, and many of them appear to like seeing people hit and hurt, which means that it is popular with the media and gets extensive coverage.

"A sport like karate or kick-boxing is highly skilled and very fast, so that it is hard to televise. In turn, that means there is little money in it, which imposes something of a handicap. We could really do with the kind of approach shown to so much sport by the Americans, who are experts at projecting it in the right way. Just look at the way they have managed to sell American football in this country, despite the absence of a British base. We need to educate the public at large in what we are doing, and to project it much more professionally. We just have to progress beyond giving demonstrations of how to smash blocks of wood with our bare hands and feet.

"At least martial arts are becoming more respectable these days. At one time they virtually existed underground, but now a lot more people are aware of them and they are becoming accepted as serious sport, and not an extension of the unarmed combat people were taught in the Armed Forces. We have a Martial Arts Commission now, and the use of things like head guards, gum shields and padding has been made compulsory. That has all helped to emphasise the technical skills involved and to remind people we are talking about a sport rather than a peacetime substitute for war. Also, martial arts have begun to be practised internationally, in a whole host of different countries. They are no longer the exclusive preserve of the Japanese".

Could a man like Lewis have sprung from another kind of environment? It seems unlikely, for the whole thrust of his campaign is towards the tough, under-privileged community of an inner city. It is that kind of community which has consistently been cited as the potential source of Britain's best sporting talent, and which tennis enthusiasts, like former Liverpool F.C. chairman John Smith have tried to exploit for the good of that game. However, Lewis has the advantage of coming from that background himself, of being a glamorous performer of international standard, and of offering a series of pastimes which are comparatively cheap and hold out the prospects of prestige among people who respect courage and strength above all else.

It is to the considerable advantage of Toxteth that he has sought to put something back into the area that gave him birth, instead of moving elsewhere to cash in on his own ability. And it is even more to his credit that he is putting such emphasis on the aspects of his chosen sport which carry the most benefits for the community as a whole. Self-discipline, self-reliance and self-help are surely the three virtues that hold out the most hope for any urban district striving to cope with the ever more commercial attitudes of the 1990s.

Since this chapter was written, Alfie Lewis has been involved in a serious late night incident in Liverpool City Centre, during which another man died. Lewis was initially charged with murder, later reduced to manslaughter, but the case had still not come to court at the time of publication. After much thought it was decided to leave the chapter in place, partly because this is intended to be an honest book which deals with people warts and all, and partly because whatever the outcome of the court case it cannot diminish the value of the work Lewis has already done for the community of Toxteth and beyond.

Gerry Marsden

If there is one song that is symbolic of Liverpool and its people it is "You'll Never Walk Alone", the hit from Carousel that was adopted by Anfield's Kop, and subsequently by most of the City, as their own personal anthem. There is no logical reason why this should have been the case, but somehow it has come to represent the unique feeling of togetherness that binds the people of Merseyside together wherever they go. Once only heard before and after football matches, it is now recognised as the most appropriate lament to be played or sung at momentous and tragic occasions, like Bill Shankly's funeral and the first gathering of the fans after the Heysel and Hillsborough Disasters.

The man almost entirely responsible for this was Gerry Marsden, singer and entertainer extraordinary, whose hoarse, highly individual voice gave what had been just another popular song a special local appeal. One of the most famous practitioners of the Mersey Sound of the Sixties, along with the Beatles, Gerry Marsden and his group, the Pacemakers, were on the crest of the wave when the record was released, but it remains as big a mystery to him as to everyone else why it made the impact it did. "It was played with a lot of other records as part of the usual pre-match entertainment" he recalls, "and for some reason the Kop picked it up, and started singing it. It caught on like wildfire, and became the Anfield signature tune almost overnight.

"Naturally I was delighted, and what made it extra nice was that with the team doing so well, it became associated with success. You used to hear it everywhere, and even now it keeps coming back at special occasions. I think one of the most moving moments was when I was married. Pauline and I are both great Liverpool fans, and we delayed going on our honeymoon to see them play Juventus in the Cup-Winners Cup on the Tuesday night. Shanks had got us seats in the directors' box and we were starting to go into it when someone shouted 'Here they are'. Next minute the whole ground took up "You'll Never Walk Alone" and sang it through twice. I have rarely been so moved and Pauline was reduced to tears. I didn't think of it at first, but I suppose it does convey this wonderful feeling of being part of the same big family, which is so important to Liverpool people.

"I think that is what probably makes Liverpool different from any other city I have been to, and believe me I have been to a good many round the world. Once you're a Scouser, either by birth or adoption, you're a Scouser for life. It doesn't matter whether the City is

In his Liverpool home, Gerry Marsden joins his fans at the Pier Head, with his back to the river that helped make Merseyside the place it is.

enjoying a boom or having a rough time, people from Liverpool are still immensely proud of the place. If you go abroad and mention you're from Liverpool, you will immediately find yourself the centre of attention, with people falling over themselves to talk to you. Say you're from Manchester or Hull or Birmingham, and nobody could care less. Say you're from Liverpool and you're asked if you know the Beatles, how Everton or Liverpool are doing, and if the Mersey Ferries are still running.

"I remember going on tour to Australia way back in 1964, and being greeted by a huge crowd at the airport. The very first person who got through security and ran up to me was a bloke called Joe, who I recognised straight away as the lad who used to stand four places from me as a kid on the Kop. It doesn't matter where you go, you will always come across Scousers. I would bet you a £10 note that if you went on a round-the-world cruise and were shipwrecked on a desert island, some guy would come up to us out of the jungle and say he was from Liverpool!

"Part of it is due to the fact that Liverpool is a port, and its people have been connected with ships and the sea for centuries. We have salt in our blood, and there can't be a family which cannot point to one or two of its members who used to go to sea. My granddad was a seaman and I know I always feel a bit nostalgic when I see the Mersey even though I'm no sailor. There used to be thousands of sailors and dockers here, and it's part of our tradition to be continually on the move. You are always hearing about the drifters in America who used to turn up in one cow town after another, and our people are much the same, only they use the sea. I have always said we are so many sea-gypsies, who love travelling to distant places and seeing strange sights, but always keep a place in our hearts for home. And I'll tell you what, the longer you are away, the more you enjoy coming back. Look what happened after Hillsborough. People all over the world rallied round because they felt the hurt personally. Even that little Aussie, Craig Johnston, flew back to Merseyside to do what he could to help, because he'd caught the feel of Liverpool".

Gerry Marsden's own roots are deep in the heart of Liverpool. He was born in Menzies Street, Dingle, close to Sefton Park with its green acres and huge tropical conservatory on the one hand, and the grim, cast-iron shore of the Mersey on the other. "I used to go down to the Cazzi (Cast Iron Shore) with Mum and swim in the river" he recalls. "I can tell you, it was bloody cold, but Mum told me to stop messing about and get in so she could have a few moments peace. When you took a dip in those days you came out with so much oil all over you that the sun couldn't get through. In fact you were more likely to catch fire than get a suntan! I tell you what, I certainly wouldn't go swimming there now, with all that I know about the water, and I certainly wouldn't let my kids swim there either. "The Mersey still looks pretty grubby to me, though they are starting to clean it up now, and I've heard that salmon have been caught in it. The thing is that we're all much better off these days, with nice new swimming pools and lots of leisure facilities that weren't there when I was a kid. The Cazzi may not have been very beautiful, but we called it the Mersey Riviera and thought it was the gear.

"The Liverpool side of the Mersey has certainly been improved so much it is hardly recognisable. It's all been cleaned up, with that lovely Albert Dock Development, lots of new houses and a posh marina. It all began with the Garden Festival, which gave Liverpool such a wonderful boost and made even people from outside realise it isn't such a bad place after all. The festival was a lot of fun, and I

85

enjoyed taking part in a concert to help get it under way, because I was so proud of what had been achieved. It was lovely to see so much enthusiasm and effort, watch thousands of people enjoying themselves, and know it had all been done by Merseysiders, with some help from outside. I think that was terribly important, and hopefully the lesson will rub off in other areas. People have to be involved in what concerns them directly if they are to develop any kind of commitment. It's no good outsiders coming in and just saying 'Do this, or do that' without asking local people what they want and what they think. I think that has been emphasised by all the problems that Liverpool Playhouse has suffered, mainly because people have come in and tried to put on productions that the paying public didn't want".

In view of his part in giving Liverpool Football Club its anthem, it seems a little surprising that Gerry Marsden originally supported their great local rivals Everton. Such a change would probably be impossible elsewhere, but it is not uncommon on Merseyside, where families love to disagree with each other, up to a point. "I switched over so I could have a good argument with the rest of the family and my friends" Gerry admits cheerfully. "Scousers love to argue with each other, because there's not much fun agreeing all the time. I started supporting Liverpool when I was 10, and soon learned that you had to find your own regular spot on the Kop, even though it is a huge terrace with nearly 20,000 people all standing there. I also learned that the one thing you must do, is keep your feet and don't try to move about, because if you once fall, you're in trouble. If you want to go to the toilet, well that's just too bad!

"The humour is unbelievable, even if you can't repeat some of the jokes in nice company. I've never laughed so much in my life as I've laughed there. No wonder people say Liverpool is a city of comedians. It's also a city of survivors, which has recovered from one tragedy after another, and at least some of that has to be due to its sense of humour. Some Scouse humour can seem a bit cruel to an outsider, but it isn't meant that way, and I think it fortifies people against the knocks they always seem to be taking.

"There has been talk about soccer being a sort of religion on Merseyside, but really I think it is more a form of therapy. For a lot of supporters, standing on the Kop is rather like going to visit a psychiatrist and being told to get rid of your inhibitions. The more you shout and cheer and complain, the better you feel, even if your team lose. And if they win, you can go home full of pride and enjoyment, ready to be friends with everyone for at least a couple of hours! I suppose a lot of people in any big city do not have a terribly

"You'll Never Walk Alone". Gerry Marsden, in Liverpool scarf, takes his place in front of the Anfield Kop.

rewarding life, especially if they are unemployed, and their local football team give them something to live for. Shanks knew just how important it was to a great many of the fans, and always drove home to his players that they were playing for the thousands up on the terraces. It may be only a game, but it is a desperately important one sometimes. You could see how involved people become after Heysel and Hillsborough. I will never forget the sight of Anfield covered in flowers after Hillsborough, as the whole city mourned for the victims".

. Gerry Marsden grew up in a musical family. His father played both the banjo and the ukelele, and his brother Fred played the drums, so it was not too surprising that he was soon both singing and playing himself. He helped to form a skiffle group when only 11, by which time he was already singing in Our Lady of Mount Carmel School choir. From skiffle he slowly graduated to Rock N'Roll, linked up with pianist Arthur McMahon, met guitarist Les Maguire in the Grapes public house, then Les Chadwick, and gradually became part of the exciting, throbbing new phenomenon, the Mersey Sound.

They had every incentive to concentrate on music. Gerry's first paying job was making tea chests at the Kardomah cafe, followed by other unglamorous duties like brushing out in Woolworths and acting as a van lad on the railway. Gerry was only 17 when the group paid their first, famous visit to Hamburg, already stirred to wild enthusiasm by the Beatles, and he soon realised where the real future lay. "Once we got started, everything began to roll and there was no question of stopping" he points out. "One thing led to another, and we had an unbelieveable time. I remember we used to play pretty well non-stop from 7 pm to 2 am, and then go night-clubbing. We sometimes felt shattered, but we could always lie in the next morning, and it was such fun we didn't really mind.

"I don't suppose anybody ever thought something like the Mersey Sound would take off in the way it did. Everyone just went wild, and it wasn't only the kids. I can recall hordes of women trying to grab me to get my clothes off! Did I mind? Certainly not — the time to get worried is when they stop wanting to! Of course we had a lot in common with the Beatles and we knew them very well because they came from the same area and we both had Brian Epstein as our manager. They were bigger than us, but we certainly didn't feel at all jealous, because we were doing very nicely too. We were all part of that fabulous Cavern Scene which made Liverpool the hub of the entertainment world for several years. Even now, more than 20 years later, people from New York to Sydney are still talking about it. I don't know if it could have happened anywhere else, but it certainly seemed to suit Liverpool, which was a very exciting place to be then. We had some marvellous tours abroad in Australia and the United States, and even appeared on the Ed Sullivan Show a couple of times, but we still enjoyed the terrific welcome we were given when we came home".

Inevitably, all good things come to an end, and close friends though they were, Gerry and his backing group, the Pacemakers eventually had to call it a day. As Gerry said later: "When you're stuck with the same guys every day for five or six years, it's a bit like being in prison. You've nothing left to say to each other'. Gerry was now married to Pauline Behan, one-time secretary of his fan club, whom he originally met at the Cavern while she was going out with

How it all began. Gerry and the Pacemakers demonstrate the clean-cut, youthful look of the Mersey Sound in the 1960s.

Beatle, George Harrison. A gifted composer, he wanted to try his hand at other forms of musical entertainment, but had no ambition to make a second film after the thoroughly enjoyable if modest "Ferry Cross the Mersey" in which he appeared with Julie Samuel, Deryck Guyler, Patricia Lawrence and Cilla Black.

His versatility was emphasised in 1968 when, to the surprise of many, he took over from Joe Brown as male lead in the popular musical "Charlie Girl" at the Adelphi Theatre, and showed a doubting world that the Liverpool pop star could also make it on the West End stage. That meant moving from his home at Caldy in Wirral to a more convenient headquarters near London and would, in some cases, have signalled the end of his interest in, and commitment to, Merseyside. Not in Gerry's. "I moved into a house owned by Frankie Vaughan (another famous Liverpool entertainer) at Sudbury on the Thames" says Gerry Marsden. "It was a nice enough place with a lovely garden, but to be honest I couldn't wait to get back home. As soon as I finished in Charlie Girl, in which I played opposite Anna Neagle and Derek Nimmo, I moved back North and felt a great deal happier. We have a lovely house in Wirral now, within easy reach of the motorway, and I couldn't be happier. It's the perfect place to bring up a couple of girls and I am close to my roots. My parents still live near Dingle, so I can visit them whenever I want, and Pauline comes from Hunt's Cross which is convenient too. It's so nice to live among sensible people, who take you as you are, and have a genuine sense of humour. They're not always trying to impress you. I suppose what I am saying really, is that Merseyside is my home, and that I feel much more comfortable here than anywhere else. I know Liverpool has its problems, but then so do most other places, and there's nothing much wrong here that cannot be put right with a bit of hard work and determination. I know one or two of the people who have made it here have left to live in more glamorous parts of the world, but I have always been proud of the place and happy to do what I can to help". That is far from being an empty phrase. Gerry Marsden has always been willing to do what he can for Liverpool and its many deserving causes over the years, in stark contrast to the lip-service paid by some other so-called celebrities. "When you love a city, you want to put things back as well as take them out", he says with impressive sincerity. "I know I have been very lucky in many ways, with my career, my marriage and my family. I suppose I might have been as successful somewhere else, because if you want something enough and work for it hard enough, it tends to happen, but I was lucky to be in Liverpool just when the Mersey Sound was sweeping the world and I was lucky that Brian Epstein was around then as well.

"Brian did a great deal for us, just as he did for the Beatles, and we owe him a tremendous debt because we were young and inexperienced, and he looked after us like a father. People in their early twenties are not into business and commerce and contracts, and it was Brian who steered us past all the pitfalls. The Mersey Sound wasn't new to us because it was heard all over Liverpool, but it was new to most other places, and that was a big asset that Brian helped us to exploit. We had a lot of fun and we made a lot of money. "My family life has been brilliant too. Pauline had Yvette quite early in our married life, but it was 13 years later that Victoria Anne arrived, when we had all but given up hope. You can graft and you can hope but you also need luck. Every now and then God smiles on you, and Victoria Anne was one of his smiles. We have so much to be thankful for".

As one of Liverpool's most distinguished sons, it was no surprise that Gerry was invited to take part in Liverpool's Royal Command Performance at the Empire Theatre, held in honour of the Queen's opening of the second Mersey Tunnel. Other Merseyside stars to sparkle in front of the Royal party were the late Rex Harrison, compere Jimmy Tarbuck, Ken Dodd, Frankie Vaughan, and the two Liverpool groups, the Scaffold and the Spinners. All in all it was an impressive display of local talent, even allowing for the many absentees, and one that merely confirmed Gerry's place in the Merseyside entertainment scene, although, in company with the others, he was just as well-known throughout the country.

That appearance was a sought-after honour, but many of Gerry's more recent concerts have had a much sadder background. He has worked tirelessly on behalf of Multiple Sclerosis, Alder Hey Children's Hospital, the Mersey Ferries, the Playhouse, the Bradford Fire Disaster Fund, and, most poignantly of all, the Hillsborough Disaster Fund. Always he has been available to help a worthy cause, either by holding a special concert, re-issuing a special record or making a very personal appearance. "I'm proud to say I am one of the Friends of the Ferries, an organisation dedicated to keeping them afloat" he says. "I suppose it was a natural connection really, after making a record and later a film called 'Ferry Cross The Mersey'. All the same it is an important cause, because what would Liverpool be without its river and its ferries? They are a vital part of our history, and even if we don't need them to cross the river these days, they enable visitors to enjoy a great view of our waterfront. And its lovely to be able to enjoy a ride across the river during your lunch break".

Alder Hey, with its fine record of helping children from all over the North West. was an obvious cause for such a patriotic Liverpudlian to support, and then came the three awful football disasters of Bradford, Heysel and Hillsborough, made even worse for Gerry Marsden because of his close connection with football and the Liverpool club. Of Heysel he says: "It hurt me as much as anyone. The people of Liverpool were as shocked as the rest of the world. They just couldn't believe what they saw on television, and they felt sick. What upset me most was that as a whole, the city that I love and the people that I love, came under such intense fire from outside. I suppose it helped to bring us all a bit closer together, but it also hurt our pride".

For the Bradford fire disaster, Gerry issued a new version of his famous song: "You'll Never Walk Alone", sung Band Aid style by a mini-Kop 68 strong, and it sold in large numbers for the appeal fund.

For services to Liverpool. Gerry Marsden, with the gold medal presented to him by Liverpool Publicity Association for his services after the Hillsborough disaster.

However, even that paled beside his non-stop efforts on behalf of the Hillsborough Disaster fund, which eventually reached the staggering total of £18 million, easily the largest sum ever raised in response to any British disaster. Totally devastated by the tragedy, he insisted on helping in every way he could, from organising concerts to making personal appeals, and none present will quickly forget his emotional singing of the Liverpool Anthem at Wembley before the F.A. Cup Final, which had many of the huge audience in tears.

It was for his work after Hillsborough that the influential Liverpool Publicity Association decided to give Gerry Marsden their prestigious annual Gold Award. Other contenders were the Royal Liverpool Philharmonic Orchestra, Falklands war hero Simon Weston (who launched the Weston Spirit in Liverpool) and Simon Yip, founder of the children's charity KIND, so Marsden's selection indicates just how highly his efforts were rated. That award was made in the May of 1990, and came only five months after another honour, a Special Scouseology Award in recognition of the £2 million raised for Hillsborough by his latest version of "Ferry Cross The Mersey".

Says Gerry: "I was very proud and honoured to be recognised by my own people in this way. Liverpool is the home of my heart, I can't say more than that. Every time I have a successful tour and am tempted to feel a little grand, Liverpool people are quick to bring me down again to a sensible level, just as they are quick to lift me if they sense something is wrong. I've always been able to go into a pub, have a drink and have a joke with the people here and I still can.

"I don't know wether the sadness we have all shared in recent years has brought us closer together, but I suspect that it has. It would be a pity if it made us more resentful of people elsewhere, or put a chip on our shoulder. It's possible that we are also feeling a bit sorry for ourselves, which would be understandable after all the knocks and disappointments. Fortunately the signs are that things are getting better, and that some of the bitterness is beginning to disappear. There are so many lovely people here, linked by their love of a great city, and I am certainly going to carry on doing my best to help them make it even greater".

From a professional point of view, Gerry's career is probably nearing the crossroads as he approaches the half-century mark. A remarkably versatile entertainer, he has appeared in variety and in pantomime as well as in clubs and concerts, adapting his act to changing circumstances and regularly touring with different groups of people. His cheerful, infectious personality has altered not at all, and he is obviously far more experienced than in his early days, but now his appeal is mainly to the older rather than the younger generation.

That hardly worries him. A wealthy man, though never ostentatious with it, he still enjoys his work immensely, and also appreciates the fact that as his commitments grow less, so he has more time left for activities like golf and, of course, for his family. "I still enjoy touring, though I don't do as much as I used to", he says. "I work when I want to, and choose what I like doing. You can't really ask more than that, can you? These days I control my own destiny, without having record producers on my back pressing me to make more and more hit records". "What does the future hold? I have no idea, but whatever it is, it will not diminish my love for, and my commitment to, Liverpool. We all need roots, a feeling that there is a place where we belong, and when you find it, it is important to cherish that connection".

Might there not be a lesson here for other distinguished sons (and daughters) of other big cities, who have achieved fame and fortune without achieving Gerry Marsden's standing in his home community and his enviable peace of mind?

John Parrott

Many men have won the World Snooker Championship and gone on to enviable fame and fortune, but one thing distinguishes the 1991 title winner from all the others. John Parrott is a Liverpudlian and proud of it. Does it really matter? After all Steve Davis comes from Romford, Alex Higgins from Belfast and Joe Johnson from Yorkshire, but that fact has not affected their form or their circumstances in any way. Davis is much better known for his ice-cool concentration than his birthplace, and Higgins for his fiery temperament and speedy play rather than his Irish background. Generally speaking it is very much a player's style and personality that determines his popularity, not where he went to school.

What makes Parrott so different is that birthplace and background *are* vitally important, not only to him, but to anyone trying to understand just what has made him such an outstanding personality.

He was born and grew up in the south end of Liverpool, like so many other successful people, was educated at New Heys Comprehensive School, and soon became an enthusiastic supporter of not just one but both the city's football clubs. That is a little unusual, since it is hard to remain a neutral long in Liverpool, but it does also underline his commitment to the city as a whole and not just one part of it. He learned to play snooker in the local clubs at the early age of 12 with the active encouragement of his father, possibly as some form of compensation for the break-up of the latter's marriage, and by his mid-teens was already so well-known to the local snooker-playing fraternity that he was being spoken of as a future champion. Long before he attracted public attention by winning the BBC's popular Junior Pot Black competition, pundits like veteran professional George Scott and league secretary Ted Robinson were predicting it would not be long before he turned professional and reached the top of his profession.

I first met Parrott when he competed in the popular Liverpool Echo pairs competiton at the age of 16, impressing even those who had not met him previously with his easy assurance, natural good manners and marked sense of humour, as well as his obvious ability with a cue. Always well dressed and well spoken, he stood out from the rest of the crowd yet, like most true champions, never seemed to do so deliberately or because he considered himself superior. Consequently, he made friends wherever he went, friends who continue to support him and enjoy his company to this day.

His natural mateyness, one of Liverpool's characteristics, has made it possible for him to mix easily, and as he says, he still likes nothing better than to pop down to the local club and play a few frames with an old friend. Indeed, he did this deliberately in the run-up to the championship that gained him his first major domestic title, reckoning that relaxed competiton against people he knew (and who received a hefty start) was one of the best possible forms of preparation. Although these days he has his own table at home to practice on whenever he wants, his natural gregariousness drives him to maintain his local links as much as is humanly possible.

This has been made easy for him because the three key people in his life, wife Karen, father Alan and manager Phil Miller are all Liverpudlians too. They have no wish to leave the city and the four have taken a conscious decision to base themselves there and use that situation to their advantage. Miller has always been a close friend and confidante, who told me many years ago: "We want John to be known as the Liverpool nice guy. He has a lovely personality, a rare ability to crack jokes spontaneously, and a natural affinity with the area. This comes over well with the general public, so it is only sensible to make use of it".

Right from the start, when he was still a successful amateur, John had his own army of supporters, who travelled long distances to give him encouragement. And in his early days as a professional, they sometimes became so enthusiastic they had to be asked to keep quiet and reminded they were watching snooker rather than football. As he won Junior Pot Black a second time and took the Pontin's Open title as an amateur, it was becoming clear he would soon be a major force to be reckoned with, despite his youth, so the travelling fans had plentiful incentive to carry on watching. Always he was only too happy to cement his relationship with the public through giving exhibitions, appearing at dinners and official functions. For two or three years, he also produced a weekly column for the Liverpool Echo in which he gave easy-to-understand tips to promising players, discussed common problems encountered in competition, and analysed the current playing situation. Far more than most young men starting out on the road to fame and fortune, he was thinking deeply about what he was doing and producing an excellent image.

Opposite:
"It's all a bit of a puzzle really". A youthful John Parrott realises he still has a lot to learn after turning professional.

When he first turned professional, he soon realised he had a great deal to learn. "It wasn't so much the shot making and potting, because I could hold my own there most of the time. It was the need for tactics, the importance of safety play and, of course, the pressure that comes when you are playing for a lot of money", he told me. "I tried to model myself on Steve Davis, because quite honestly, he is the best there is. I have always admired him for his behaviour and conduct of himself as much as for his actual playing. He is the complete professional, and you can't say much better than that. Steve does lose sometimes, though not very often, and he is always the man to beat. Even when you think you have got him, you are liable to find that you haven't".

At 18, George Scott had remarked: "I don't think there is anyone around who can teach John anything. He has amazing ability, and all he needs now is experience. He certainly has the potential to become a world champion". That was a remarkable tribute, but only partially true, because at that stage John could not really cope with all the pressure. When he reached his first major semi-final, in the Lada Classic at neighbouring Warrington, he was actually relieved to be beaten, though naturally disappointed too. "Thank God for that", he remarked at the post-match interview. "I knew before I went to the table that I was not ready for a final yet. With the crowd and the television and the sense of occasion, it is still a bit too much".

With the increased commercialisation of sport, and the expansion of snooker world-wide, most leading players are now signed up by high-powered agents like Barry Hearn, who guarantee them vast amounts of money through exhibition matches, endorsements and all the other trappings of sporting success. John Parrott duly joined the 'stable' of Ian Doyle, who then had Stephen Hendry and several other leading players under contract, but split with him after it became clear Doyle did not see eye to eye with Phil Miller. "With his personality, John should be doing far better and making far more money than he is", said Doyle. "The trouble is, I have never been given the chance to promote him properly". Parrott and Miller said very little, but after a spell with Howard Kruger, they broke away from the big boys entirely and have since campaigned independently. "Phil knows me, and I know him", says John simply. "We know what we're doing, and we're both happy, which is the important thing".

Surprisingly for a young man of such obvious talent, it has taken John Parrott quite a long time to reach the top. Although age is no real barrier to success, with former world champion Fred Davis still going strong in his seventies, modern snooker is basically a young man's game, and many new arrivals enjoy success at an early stage. Neal Foulds, and Stephen Hendry in particular wasted no time challenging the best when they turned professional, but Parrott's progress has been much more measured, though it is possible he will stay up there rather longer now he has finally got to the top. "When I first turned professional it was roses all the way", he recalls. "You find yourself in super halls and playing on far better tables than you've played on previously, and to begin with you just can't go wrong. You are not expecting to win anything, so every time you beat a leading player it is a nice surprise. You go for the shots, and never think about what will happen if you miss.

"Then after a season or so, you begin to realise just how hard it is to keep winning consistently, and how many good players there are around. Your own ranking has improved, so you are expected to do better, and if you are not careful you start to think about not losing rather than actually winning. That is a fatal attitude to have, because above all else in snooker you must be positive. The thing I found was that there is just no substitute for experience. When I played people like Davis and Terry Griffith I knew I could pot almost as well as them, but their positional and safety play was in a different league, and I kept on making silly mistakes".

Even so, Parrott did not do at all badly, and his world ranking kept on improving, although he never seemed able to actually win anything, at least in this country. His first outright victory came during a tour of the Far East, when he won the Chinese Open and found himself an international celebrity in a country that had only taken up snooker recently. "It was a wonderful trip and an experience I certainly will not forget in a hurry", he says. "I loved visitng places like the Great Wall and one or two of the old palaces, but everything seemed terribly crowded and I've never seen so many bikes in my life.

"I don't want to sound rude, because they were very nice people, but the food was terrible. I remember sitting down to a big formal banquet and being offered raw sea slug. It was horrible. I had to keep making excuses to get up and go to the toilet; they must have thought I had trouble with my bladder. One of the main highlights of the week for many people was a meal out at McDonalds. Yes they've got one in Peking, or Beijing as they call it now. People got themselves all dressed up for a night out there, which tells you something about what was on offer everywhere else. Of course we were playing against much the same people we play at home, since they have not developed any outstanding players of their own yet, but the atmosphere was eerie. We played in dead silence, punctuated by sudden bouts of hand-clapping, and I'm not sure they really appreciated what were the best shots".

John's next tournament wins were also abroad, and included two in the European Open. After the first, he couldn't wait to get back to Liverpool and parade his handsome new trophy at the annual Merseyside Sports Personality of the Year awards dinner, "just to prove that I really can win something!" It was certainly a welcome success, but one he would willingly have swopped for victory in one

A trophy at last! John Parrott with the trophies awarded him after his first major championship in the Chinese Open.

of the many domestic tournaments, because back in England he seemed fated to be ever the bridesmaid and never the bride. Having eventually managed to beat the great Steve Davis occasionally, and end the feelings of awe in which he held him. Parrott now found another major barrier in the person of Stephen Hendry. "He's just unbelievable. He *would* turn up now that I've come to terms with Steve", John said with feeling. "I've not been playing badly myself, but some of his form has been simply unbelievable. Some people have said I haven't got the bottle for a really big match, or that I can't handle a tight contest. That is ridiculous. The truth is that I invariably seem to catch either Steve or Stephen when one of them is red hot".

That certainly seemed to be true, but at the same time one felt that Parrott was not helping his cause by taking what often looked like unnecessary risks at vital moments in the biggest matches. With the frame at his mercy, he would be tempted into going for a near-impossible shot, to miss it and let his opponent back in.

The year of 1989 proved to be a major turning point in Parrott's career. He was now among the top four players in the world and showing great consistency, although still having to concede top spot to his two great rivals. It looked as though he might achieve the break-through in the world championships, as he played with more and more conviction, but sadly it all went sour in the final when he was crushed 18-3 by Davis in one of the most one-sided contests the tournament had ever seen. Typically, there were no excuses, only a comment that his grandmother could have given him a start and won, but deep down he was badly hurt by the magnitude of his defeat, and the freely-voiced suggestions that he lacked the tough streak needed by a champion.

"People say I should try and be nastier, that I should develop a touch of ruthlessness and start hating my opponents, at least during the match, but that is ridiculous", he told me afterwards. "Basically, I think I am a nice person. I like other people and admire them if they do well. I have tried being hard but it doesn't work for me, and it would be silly to try and be something I am not. I suppose it may look as if I'm not doing my best when I crack a joke at an interview, but that comes naturally to me and is really just a means of relaxing the tension inside.

"Look at Dennis Taylor. He may look all nice and cuddly behind those huge glasses, but don't let that fool you. He is a very tough competitor, who fights all the way. He likes a laugh as much as anyone, but he doesn't let that affect his concentration, and it's just the same with me. If I'm losing matches there is only one reason, and that is that I am not playing well enough and not making the right decisions at critical moments. There is also another factor which may come into it, though I don't want to sound as though I'm making excuses. These days there are a great many different tournaments all over the country, with one starting as the one before finishes, and if you are having a successful time, you tend to be involved in all of them. I had been playing pretty well in the spring, been involved in a lot of tough matches, and was starting to feel very tired. By the time I had finished at the Crucible I was like a wet rag, completely worn out. I tell you snooker can be a very demanding game".

John had extra special reasons for wanting to win in 1989. He was due to marry his childhood sweetheart, Karen Tasker, shortly afterwards, and he also wanted to do something tangible for the people of Liverpool, still in shock from the Hillsborough football disaster. A fan of both clubs, he had actually gone to watch Everton rather than Liverpool in the other semi-final but could so easily have witnessed the horror live rather than seeing it recorded on televison later. "I was too shocked to take it in", he told me. "I grew up on the terraces of the Kop and Gwladys Street, and have many friends on both. Some of the victims were people I knew and I feel as upset as anybody not directly involved. Human life is so much more important than a snooker match or two, but I hope that any success I do achieve will help to make one or two people feel a little bit better".

Fortunately he still had his wedding to look forward to, plus setting up home for the first time in his own house. He loved every minute of it, though confessed happily that his entire life was now in a state of chaos. "I've never felt better, but I'm in a bit of a shambles at the moment", he told me. "I've got my own billiard table, but the room is so full of other furniture that I can't get into it to practice. Every time I try to pot a black I'm snookered. It's lovely to have somewhere of my own to come home to, and find my wife has put out the slippers. The only thing is that I have still got to work out a new routine that enables me to fit everything in properly.

"I have been looking forward to this for a very long time, and I'm going to make the most of it. I would like a lot of kids because I am an only child myself, and even though I had all the love in the world when I was growing up I still think I must have missed something. I

Opposite:
On the ball and on his way to victory. John Parrott heads for another victory on his way to the World Championship.

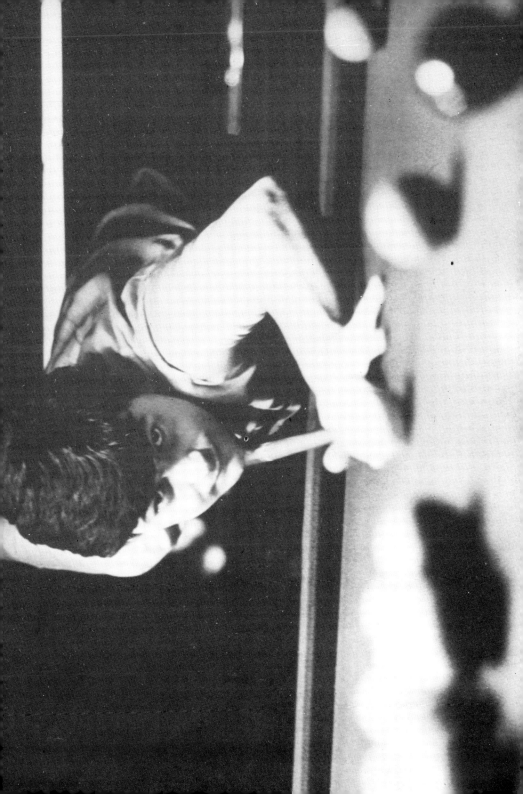

have this picture of family breakfasts with cereal all over the place and confusion everywhere. I know it sounds corny, but I mean it. I'm very much a home bird at heart. Karen doesn't come to all my matches, but she is usually at the really big ones, and it means an awful lot to me. I notice that Steve Davis has stopped winning quite so often since he got married himself, so I suppose it could affect my game, but that's a risk I'm only too happy to take".

In fact the next season was not a particularly successful one for John, who continued to be a "nearly" man, but the autumn of 1990 saw him running into much better form. With his own billiard table nicely set up at home, and a new domestic routine firmly established, he seemed set for stardom and picked up two more overseas titles in the Belgian and Monaco Grand Prix. "I don't know why my results are better abroad, perhaps it's something to do with my brand of Continental aftershave", he joked. Two more defeats followed in domestic finals, which led him to quip, tongue in cheek: "I'm a bit like Everton, I can't win at home".

Part of the trouble was undoubtedly the dominance of Hendry, who had now taken over from Davis as world number one and was showing magnificent form, but at least Parrott was being well rewarded for coming second. After losing to Hendry in the final of the Benson and Hedges tournament, in which he had previously beaten Davis 5-1, Parrott produced another of his pearls: "I'd go out and get a proper job tomorrow, but where else could I pick up £38,000 for coming second", he asked. "The problem is not that I am playing badly, but that Stephen is bursting with confidence. He feels he can't miss, and at the moment he's right". As the year ended, Parrott began to have trouble with his cue. "It doesn't feel right", he explained. "A cue is such a vital thing to a snooker player, that it has to be perfect, so well balanced that you are not even aware of it. This is an old cue that I've had for a long time, and I suppose it has taken quite a battering". Frustrated by a couple of shock defeats, John sent the cue away for repairs, but it never felt quite the same again. "I had various bits and bobs added but I was never happy with it, so I ordered a new one", he explained later. "When it arrived it felt strange at first, then I had one or two small adjustments made, and now it feels fine. A cue has to be like an extension to your body, so that you can concentrate 100 per cent on the balls and what you want to do with them. If you are thinking about your cue, you are in big trouble. The only snag is that now my cue is O.K. again, I have not got many matches in which to use it. I was having so much trouble early in the year that I didn't qualify for the events leading up to the World Championship, so instead of getting plenty of match play I am having to rely on practice at home".

As in all the best novels and plays, all came right on the night. During his build-up to Sheffield, John was virtually forced to take plenty of rest and arrived there fresher than he had been for a major tournament in years. And if he had gone short of match practice, with the exception of some light-hearted handicap matches with old friends at the local clubs, he was running into quite unbelievable form at home. "I'm knocking in century breaks like there was no tomorrow", he told me shortly before leaving for the Crucible. "I doubt if I have ever hit the ball so cleanly". Manager Miller also called in former world champion John Spencer for a few words of tactical advice, so when the Championships began, Parrott was perfectly prepared, if still an outsider in the betting.

That continued to be the case even after he had claimed a couple of valuable scalps on an unpublicised march towards the final. All the attention was focussed on Davis and Hendry, with Jimmy White suddenly emerging as favourite to beat them both after some spectacular displays. Then suddenly it was the final, with an inspired White due to meet a Parrott determined to atone for his previous humiliation by Davis two years previously. The rest, as they say, is history. Playing calm, measured snooker, potting every ball in sight but refusing to take the slightest risk, John virtually assured himself of the title by taking the first seven frames without reply, as a shattered White could only sit and watch. The spectators all agreed, they had never seen snooker like it, and even a happy Parrott admitted later: "I doubt if I will ever be able to play like that again. I just couldn't miss, and I even felt sorry for Jimmy".

White did fight back, very creditably, but the handicap was far too great, and after trailing 5-11 at the end of the first day, he eventually went down 11-18. Well in front, Parrott was content to sit tight and make his opponent take the risks, while he waited to pounce. He had, after all, no need to prove anything after that fantastic display on the first morning, which had pretty well ensured that the "nearly" man of so many years ago would win his first major British title in the biggest event of them all.

Needless to say, Parrott couldn't get to sleep after his victory. All hyped-up and with the adrenalin pumping, he was up and pacing round his Sheffield hotel by 6 am the next morning. "The trouble with sleeping was that winning might have seemed too much like a dream", he joked. "I still cannot really believe it, but I am so pleased for everyone who has helped me, as well as for myself. At least, I have shown that I am capable of beating the best, and that I'm not 'too nice' to get anywhere".

Two of Liverpool's world champions. John Parrott and Kirkby boxer Paul Hodkinson show off some of the awards they won in 1992. In Hoko's case that meant a world championship belt rather than a cup.

Highlights of the subsequent celebrations were, inevitably, a civic reception at Liverpool Town Hall and the parading of his Championship trophy in front of the Kop before the start of Liverpool's final league match with Spurs. "That was something I shall always remember with pride", he says with understandable pride. "It was lovely to bring back at least one piece of silverware to the city after all the disappointments (on the football field) and to feel I had done at least one little thing for Liverpool. In fact, Parrott has done much, much more for his beloved city. He gave exhibitions and supported appeals in aid of the Hillsborough Disaster Fund, played a prominent part in the other major appeal in support of Alder Hey Hospital, and has often turned up unexpectedly to cheer children suffering from serious illness. Typical was an incident in 1990, when he paid a special visit to 6-year-old cerebral palsy victim Andrew Wright of Kirkby, who returned home with his parents from a visit to the Peto Institute in Hungary to find his home ransacked. Handing over an autographed cue, Parrott told the youngster: "Never give in. You've got to keep on working", advice which Wright has taken very much to heart. Similarly, he staged a special exhibition for the benefit of cancer victim Graham Potts, as a part of his continued commitment to the community.

Not even Parrott knows what the future holds, but in his case it looks a rosy one. A happy marriage and a successful career give promise of great things to come, though it is possible that, in order to keep his competitive edge, he may have to cut down on at least some of his expanding commitments. "If you try to do too much, or make too much money, you will probably end up half killing yourself and being miserable", he says with total commonsense. A level-headed young man, with his feet still firmly on the ground, John Parrott is a credit to the city that has given him standards to be proud of.

Councillor Harry Rimmer

No book about Liverpool people would be complete without the inclusion of at least one representative of positive, caring Socialism. Not the blind, near revolutionary fanaticism symbolised by the Militant Tendency, which also has its roots in the city, but the much more realistic yet far less publicised struggle on behalf of the under-dog waged with such vigour by heroic figures like Bessie and John Braddock shortly after World War Two, and carried on by the likes of Eric Heffer and Bill Sefton. Those were people of massive stature, respected by even their opponents, who were only interested in power as a means of achieving a better deal for the poor and the underpriviledged, and would sacrifice almost anything to achieve it.

Liverpool's contribution to the trade union movement has been equally impressive, and is symbolised by former TG and W leader Jack Jones, who supported the cause of freedom so strongly that he actually fought in the Spanish civil war and was wounded in the process. In later years, Liverpool docker Jones moved into the Midlands, but he has always remained a Liverpudlian at heart, whether fighting casualisation in the docks or, in more recent years, battling to get a better deal for pensioners.

Today, the mantle of Heffer, Jones and the Braddocks has fallen on the broad shoulders of Councillor Harry Rimmer, the man charged with the unenviable task of sorting out Liverpool's finances, repairing at least some of the damage caused by chaotic years of extremist policy, and persuading a disillusioned populance to face reality. At the time of writing, he could not rely on a majority of his own party for unquestioning support, and faced the upsetting prospect of being regarded as a class traitor by many of those he was seeking to help. The striking parallel with Soviet leader Mikhail Gorbachev is unmistakable. Like Gorbachev, he has been trying to move a part of society into a world with which they are unfamiliar, like Gorbachev he has tried to talk to all factions in an effort to bring them together, and like Gorbachev, he is in constant danger of being stabbed in the back by the people he has done most for and whom he trusts the most. "I just hope things don't become quite so explosive as they have in the Soviet Union", he jokes. "It's bad enough having burning rags thrust through the letter box in your flat, but at least we are unlikely to see tanks cruising down the streets of Liverpool".

Brought up in Liverpool by a staunch working class family, Harry Rimmer was educated at the former Liverpool Collegiate School, and took an immediate interest in local politics. Like most young men he was a bit of a firebrand, wanting to change the world within a week, and became friendly with many of Merseyside's leading Socialists. "There is nothing very new about the Militants", he says. "Long before they were heard of, the city was the home of international socialism and full of near revolutionaries. I grew up with all the right slogans. It was only much later that I learned it is deeds not words that matter".

By 1952, when he was in his early twenties, Rimmer had won a seat on Liverpool City Council, but he held it for only a year, partly because of major ward reorganisation, but mainly because his health suddenly deteriorated. "I went down with tubercolosis, and spent most of the next two years in a sanatorium", he explains. "These days, they generally treat TB with drugs, but then they still believed in operating, and I had a third of my right lung removed. When I came out of hospital, there was no time for politics. I was married (to Joan) and had a young family to care for, so I concentrated on finding and keeping a job (as an electrician) which has never been too easy in Liverpool.

"However I wasn't entirely inactive, because I was always a strong union man, and I reckon I must have held every unpaid union post over the years. I became factory convenor at the U.K. Atomic Energy plant at Capenhurst for five years, and was right in the middle of the long drawn-out negotiations over redundancies there, as chairman of the joint shop stewards committee. That was a tough time, but I suppose even then I realised that you don't get very far by blind confrontation. I am a great believer in negotiation, and I will talk to anyone.

"By 1981 things had changed at home, and I returned to local government as a member of the old Merseyside County Council in 1981, being elected deputy leader the following year. That only lasted until 1986, when the county council was wound up, and I still believe that was a great mistake. The metropolitan councils had a major contribution to make, and were able to achieve something strategic on behalf of the whole conurbation. There was far too much fragmentation after local government was reorganised, with too many bodies that were too small to stand on their own feet properly. Knowsley is a good example. It is much too small to provide a proper education service all on its own.

"It would have been much better to keep the county councils and give them additional responsibility over education and social services. There would have been a far wider educational base, providing a better range of services for all, and of course it is a big advantage to have education and transport under the same roof.

"Why can't they get to the point?" Harry Rimmer waits for rational argument to begin again in Liverpool's Council chamber.

That also applies to the social services, because you need to control public transport if you want to provide a proper service for the sick and the elderly. Unfortunately the county councils were not popular with the Tory Government, who wanted to keep closer control on their spending, and get full credit for it". Moving onto the newly reconstituted City Council plunged Harry Rimmer into a very different world, where confrontation, not consultation was the rule. "On the County Council, the representatives of the various parties had respect for each other and co-operated for the good of the area", he recallss. "We could disagree over policy and campaign against each other, but it was done in a relatively civilised way. I have to say that it disgusts me to listen to some of the argument in the Liverpool council chamber, which is often based on one person trying to shout down the other. Also, although I am not a snob, I believe there should be a basic standard of behaviour by people who are representing a part of the city. It hurts me to see councillors putting their feet up on the seats, or chewing crisps and drinking cans of coke in the council chamber. Democracy is all about public debate, but there is not a lot of point in putting forward a reasoned argument if people are not prepared to listen".

Strangely enough, Harry Rimmer is still very much a believer in an open door policy, and is never too busy (or too grand) to speak to anybody. "I have said I am a great believer in democracy, and I mean that", he stresses. "Someone once advised Parliament 'Trust the people' and he was right. In my experience, the majority view of any given situation is usually the right one, always provided they have been given the right information on which to make their judgement. We have seen the effect of this in regard to the Poll Tax and again in the Soviet Union recently. In Liverpool, Militancy survived while a majority were prepared to let it happen in the hope it would produce some kind of a miracle. Now, I hope, the majority are starting to realise the necessity of co-operation with other people".

How much Rimmer suffered during the extremist regime of Tony Byrne, Derek Hatton and Tony Mulhearn, none will ever know. "I opposed what they were doing, but they were in the majority", he points out. "Since 1983 successive Labour councils have tried to answer their problems by confrontation, on the basis that if they made themselves a big enough nuisance, someone would step in to bale them out. That does not work because, as I have always maintained, Parliament can do what it likes. We live in a Parliamentary democracy which is the envy of the world, and under that system no city can dictate policy to central government, or try to overthrow their policy through any other method than by use of the ballot box.

"Neil Kinnock was right when he said: "Law makers must never be law breakers". Whether you like Government policy or not is immaterial. You must abide by it, or we would be plunged into a state of anarchy. Where you have a situation in which a city is controlled by a party of a different persuasion from the one in control of Parliament, you must use all your skills and all your bargaining ability to make use of the opportunities that are provided to obtain additional resources".

"Neil Kinnock was right." Harry Rimmer greets his friend and then party leader on the latter's visit to Liverpool during the Militant crisis.

In 1987, when 47 Militants were banned from the Council, Harry Rimmer took over the official Labour leadership for a brief six months. "Nearly all our worst problems stem from the weakness of our financial base, so I wanted to start an immediate dialogue with Government to see what additional resources were available through things like inner city grants and land grants", he explains.

"I also wanted re-determination of our committed expenditure, because I thought there was a real danger that the Secretary of State might give us additional money, but attach conditions to its use that would not be acceptable. I had several 'unofficial' meetings with Nicholas Ridley and David Trippier, and was given 'unofficial' assurances that we would receive additional cash without the imposition of sanctions. I was delighted, thinking I had achieved a real break-through, but my fellow Labour Group members disagreed and voted against it. I had every reason to think the Government would be helpful, because they wanted to demonstrate that if a Labour council behaved reasonably, in their view, they could be reasonable too".

Rimmer was succeeded as leader of the City Council by Keva Coombes, who held office for two years before resigning in May 1990. In stepped Harry Rimmer again, even though he admitted at the time that: "I see nothing but problems ahead". And what problems there were. Liverpool had teetered to the brink of bankruptcy, and there was an acute financial crisis, made even more acute by the failure of the city's work force to realise that it was no longer possible to operate whole departments as a branch of the social services. Not only were many councillors now working full time and living on their expenses, as opposed to the old fashioned idea of acting as volunteers, but over-staffing had reached a ridiculous level because it was used as a means of compensation for job cuts elsewhere.

"Compared with other, similar cities there is no doubt we are over-staffed", Rimmer admitted on retaking office. "It was from the best reasons, common humanity, but it cannot go on. For years now, all political parties have allowed over-staffing to prevail because we have been loath to add to the city's unemployment problems. This issue has got to be addressed now, if we are to have a City Council which provides efficient, value for money services, without having an astronomically high poll tax. To make a legal budget, we have to cut our spending by £26.6 million, and it is impossible to do that without reducing staff substantially".

The legislation that brought the issue of over-manning directly to a head, and which Rimmer tacitly admits was fully justified, was that requiring Compulsory Tendering for all council services. Suddenly, each department's services have become subject to detailed scrutiny, illustrating that in some cases at least, Liverpool rates and poll tax payers have not been getting value for money. First to be highlighted was the refuse collection service or, to quote many frustrated

Liverpudlians, the refuse non-collection service, whose failure to keep the city even reasonbly clean had become the subject of non-stop complaint from numerous quarters.

"After CCT was announced, I warned the union at least 12 months in advance of what was going to happen", emphasises Harry Rimmer. "A District Auditor's survey had shown that our refuse collection service was not only the most expensive of any comparable city in the country, but the least efficient. I told the union leaders they would have to agree to reorganisation to have any hope of winning the tender, and after some argument they agreed. Then, on the very first day they were due to operate the new, streamlined system, they went on unofficial strike! I ask you, what can you do in that kind of situation?

"When they put in their tender, I was told: "When (not if) you award it to us, don't forget there will be an extra £300,000 due to us for operating the new system, which is not in the tender. I just couldn't believe it, and neither could David Plunkett (former head of Sheffield City Council) when I told him. In the event, our department's tender was double the one submitted by the French firm Onyx. However much we might have wanted to help our own people, there was just nothing we could do".

A similar situation affected other council departments, which had also been operating for several years at much less than maximum efficiency. The ground maintenance service, for example, lost £800,000 over the first two phases of its programme to put its entire future in doubt, and there are others with good cause to wonder what will happen to them.

"We are paying the penalty now for fudging the issue over the last eight to ten years", says Councillor Rimmer. "The city's problems have got deeper and deeper because of our poor financial base. There have been a succession of budgets which have purported to balance the books by so-called 'Creative accounting', an undue reliance on capital receipts and a refusal to come to terms with staffing levels. In 1990, when I became leader, I realised we could not continue to rely on capital receipts, because most of Liverpool's most marketable assets had already been sold. In any case, I believe that the whole policy of selling the family silver, as Harold McMillan called it, is open to serious question, because those assets are a valuable part of Liverpool's heritage and, in many instances, affects the quality of people's lives".

Successive legislation has made it much more difficult to continue following the traditional policy of robbing Peter to pay Paul, that is, moving money around from one area to another. The introduction of

Compulsory Competitive Training has meant that each department now has to produce its own budget, which must balance in its own right, and has killed stone dead one of Liverpool's former practices which involved diverting money intended for a variety of other things, into the housing account. "By law, we now have to produce a separate mini-budget for housing", says Harry Rimmer, "and that has to take in the cost of repair work as well. When you realise that in the past the housing department was subsidised by literally millions of pounds, you can understand how grim the situation has become.

"The first thing we had to do was put up council house rents, and of course that is an intensely emotive and unpopular thing to do. Liverpool had applied a rent-freeze since 1983, and make no mistake it was fully justified then. There had been a series of steep increases previously, which had left Liverpool's council rents the highest outside London. At the time I was 100 per cent in support. Unemployment was high, there was little money about and we had to try and help the poorest section of the community. But to think we could maintain that situation was ridiculous. Nobody could reasonably expect us to keep such a freeze going indefinitely, especially after several years of high inflation. By 1990, Liverpool's rents were lower than those of every other city except Leeds, and even there it was only a matter of a few pence. We had no choice but to put ours up, and look into the possibility of achieving agreement over private house building. "I hope we shall be able to do one or two deals with private companies over some of the large stocks of derelict housing in our possession. It makes no sense at all to leave them lying empty when lots of people are in need of homes. What I have in mind is an agreement under which the builders would agree to repair the derelict property and bring it up to a good living standard, in return for permission to build a limited number of new houses for sale to owner occupiers. In that way, I think we might be able to enjoy the best of both worlds".

Posterity may accord Harry Rimmer a leading place in Liverpool's history, as an enlightened statesman who had the courage to stand fast against disreputable practice, but he is getting precious little appreciation in his own home town. "We talked about the similarity of my situation and President Gorbachev's. Well here is another good example", he says, with more than a hint of typical Liverpool humour. "Gorbachev became a hero in the West, with Britain and the United States queueing-up to pay tribute to him, but he soon became extremely unpopular within the Soviet Union. There, his reforms have still to bear fruit, and he has taken the blame for the faults of his predecessors, which have left the Soviet economy in a dreadful state.

"I am trying to do my best for the people of Liverpool, and to persuade them that the habits of the past just will not work, but it is not a very pleasant task. I am having to make hundreds of people redundant, and thousands of others pay higher rents, because I know that if I don't the city will become bankrupt. You can hardly expect those on the receiving end to be happy about it, but I do wish they understood the need for what is happening. If we had grasped the nettle eight or ten years ago, a lot of this unhappiness might have been avoided, and the city as a whole would have been in a much stronger position. Typically, I get plenty of support from outside. I have received many letters of congratulation from people in other towns and cities, who have no doubt about the value of what I am trying to do.

"It is not very nice when Liverpool people shout rude comments at you, or label you a 'traitor' or a 'Judas'. Even some of those whom I used to think of as being among my closest friends, now refuse to speak to me, or only do so reluctantly. Do they think I enjoy carrying out unpopular measures which cause hardship? Sometimes you would think they do. I have even been labelled a Thatcherite or a 'Tory lackey', which is ridiculous, because I dislike all that the Tories and Margaret Thatcher stand for as much as they do. I hate the Poll tax and privatisation and many of the other things they have introduced, but the cold fact of life is that we all have to live with them. And you don't have very convincing grounds for objecting to certain facets of Tory policy, when your own city's record in some areas is so appalling. How could we argue against privatisation of rubbish collection, when our department had performed so badly and given such a poor service?"

Popularly known as "Unflash Harry" because of his down to earth approach and dislike of cheap publicity, Harry Rimmer could hardly be less like the notorious Derek Hatton, who ran the city for so many disastrous years. He refuses to discuss his predecessor, who was of course technically deputy leader to Councillor John Hamilton, but makes it clear he has no use at all for what Hatton represented. "I am a devoted Socialist of what I would call the old school, who has devoted my life to the Labour Party", he emphasises. "But I am also an unashamed pragmatist, who realises that you have to give and take in order to achieve things. My aim, and the aim of those who support me, is quite simply to find the best available solutions to our problems and obtain the best possible deal for the people of Liverpool who elected me.

"We have to live in the real world, and not become so isolated that we start thinking we should be treated differently from everyone else.

"I'll talk to anyone if it will help." Harry Rimmer (right) joins Tory Minister Michael Heseltine and Liberal leader Sir Trevor Jones at the conference table.

We can make our case to Parliament, when we apply for grants, but there will be others also making their case, and ours has to be more convincing than theirs if it is to succeed. Slick slogans like "No rate increases to pay for Tory cuts" may sound convincing, but they don't actually achieve anything. In the end, we still have to find the money from somewhere to balance the books. And we also have to convince a lot of people outside Merseyside, not just in Parliament, but in industry and commerce too, that we are a reponsible body who can be trusted.

"How can we expect people to invest here, or bring new businesses into Liverpool, if they are not sure whether the Council's leaders will deal fairly and honestly with them? I have no doubt that Liverpool's reputation suffered very badly during the eighties because of the Council's attitude, and there are a lot of fences to be repaired. I may be a bit of an optimist by nature, but I am confident that things are beginning to move in Merseyside's favour at long last. Recovery is only just round the corner, provided we don't mess things up ourselves. The MDC and the City Challenge Initiative have both brought us a lot of benefits and it is vital we make the best use of our other resources."

Although it doesn't always show, Harry Rimmer is an emotional man. He has been reduced to tears at the end of some particularly bitter debates, and has already threatened to resign once since reassuming the leadership. "I have to say there remains the very real danger that the Labour Group on the City Council will break down, if we are not careful", he admits. "We are only in a minority at the moment, and it is quite possible that the left wingers, or the reactionaries or even the Liberals will manage to throw me out. Why do I carry on, amidst all the aggro? Well I said before that I have rather old-fashioned values, and those include seeing a job through to the bitter end, whatever the difficulties.

"I learned early on that there are people who make fine speeches, and people you can trust. I suppose one of the arts of leadership lies in telling one from the another. I have also learned that no group and no party has a monopoly of wisdom or genuinely good intentions. There are as many bloody-minded and obstructive people among the workers as there are among the bosses. You have to make up your own mind to do what you believe to be right, regardless of the personal consequences.

"I suppose in the end it is the thought of doing something worthwhile for my native city of Liverpool that drives me on. We are roughly 10 years behind some other parts of the country, but when we do catch up, they had better watch out! "So often in the past, other cities have learned from our experience, and I know the whole country was keeping an eye on our encounter with the Militants to see what would happen. They are probably wondering now whether we have come through the crisis. I only hope that the people of Liverpool are ready to show them that we have".

Peter Robinson

The names of Liverpool and Everton are synonymous with football, and a great many people beyond the confines of Merseyside often seem to think it dominates everything else in the area. Certainly it is impossible for anyone residing for any length of time within five miles of the Pier Head to avoid stating his allegiance to one club or the other, and even the Archbishop of Liverpool has admitted that to many it is a form of religion. There is nothing new in all this, for records show that similar enthusiasm existed even before the First World War. What is comparatively new is the way in which the two great clubs have dominated the domestic soccer scene over the last 30 years.

The arrival of John (later Sir John) Moores as chairman of Everton and an influential, behind-the-scenes figure at Liverpool, was followed by the appointment of two great managers in Harry Catterick and Bill Shankly, which triggered off an astonishing renaissance, the results of which live on today. Looking back, most supporters remember with pride and affection the names of managers like the two just mentioned, plus those of Bob Paisley and Howard Kendall, and a whole host of outstanding players like Kevin Keegan, Kenny Dalglish, Trevor Steven, Peter Reid, Ian Rush and Neville Southall. Few stop to think of the immense contribution made by the club's chief executives, Jim Greenwood of Everton and above all, the quiet man of Anfield. Peter Robinson.

Peter Robinson's arrival could hardly be termed auspicious, for he succeeded a former Liverpool player, Jimmy McInnes, who had died in tragic circumstances. That was in the spring of 1965, when Liverpool had just won the F.A. Cup for the first time, and were roaring forward on the crest of a wave propelled by the Beatles music. In his very first season, the new man saw his club win the League Championship and reach the final of the European Cup Winners Cup, while on the other side of Stanley Park, Everton were following them as winners of the F.A. Cup. The pair met in the Charity Shield at the start of the next season, and were led out by Roger Hunt and Ray Wilson respectively, who had just helped England to win the World Cup. It could hardly have been a harder act to follow.

Amazingly, things got even better. Although Merseyside has suffered acute economic decline and lost many of its population, its two major clubs have defied logic by winning almost as many trophies as everyone else put together. In the 19 seasons beginning

Nothing but the best, please. Chairman Sir John Smith, manager Bob Paisley and chief executive Peter Robinson watch Kenny Daglish, arguably the finest footballer ever to play for Liverpool, signing on the dotted line.

with the birth of Shankly's second great team in 1972-73, Liverpool won the First Division title 11 times and finished runners-up seven. The only season they fell below second place was that of 1980-81, and even then they enjoyed the considerable consolation of winning both European and League Cups!

Nor have Everton been exactly idle. Until George Graham's Arsenal broke their near-monopoly with that most sensational of all victories at Anfield soon after Hillsborough, the Championship had remained on Merseyside for seven full seasons, with Howard

Kendall's side taking the title twice. Everton also appeared in four F.A. Cup finals in six seasons between 1984-89, and of course were Cup Winners Cup holders when the Heysel tragedy brought European competition to a temporary end.

Talk of Europe, reminds one of Liverpool's astonishing record there too. For 21 years in succession, they qualified to play in one or other of the major competitions, and their last nine challenges before that ban after Heysel, were all in the European Cup itself, an event they have already won four times.

Such statistics may make heavy reading, but they do illustrate the remarkable achievements of two fine clubs, Liverpool in particular, in the face of intense competition. And as Peter Robinson emphasises: "What our joint records prove, is that given the right management and employees, it is possible to run a consistently successful business on Merseyside. Neither of our clubs has enjoyed any special advantages, and we have both competed for players with everyone else. With the exception of the footballers, who have come from many different sources, we have always insisted on employing local people, most of whom have stayed with us for the bulk of their lives. We have always believed that the people of Liverpool are among the most dependable in the country, and both our employees and our supporters have proved us right time and again".

So what is the secret of the Mersey Masters? Has it been generous financial backing, the presence of a permanent pool of outstanding players, or some other factor peculiar to Merseyside? Robinson believes it has all been down to realism, continuity and, above all, good management. "I cannot emphasise too strongly the impact that Sir John Moores' influence has had on both clubs", he stresses. "He did not have a direct involvement with Liverpool, but he was able to give us invaluable advice in a great many ways. He was a close friend of our former chairman T. V. Williams, the man who brought Bill Shankly to Anfield, and of our recent chairman Sir John Smith, but probably his greatest contribution was in seconding one of the Littlewoods Directors, Eric Sawyer, to serve on our board when we were starting to reorganise. It was Eric Sawyer who persuaded the board that if they wanted success, they must insist on getting the best, and pushed them into making the money available for the signing of players like Ian St John and Ron Yeats.

"That policy proved successful in a spectacular way, and so ever-afterwards a Liverpool manager has always been able to bid for the players he wants, provided they are available or not being offered at a ridiculous price. The club have never spent money for the sake of it, but they have been willing to invest in outstanding players because, as Sir John once said, a football club's real assets are out on the pitch".

Peter Robinson also points to the fact that, unlike so many other big clubs, both Liverpool and Everton have enjoyed stability both on and off the field. "There have been no battles for power at either club", he explains. "Directors have generally remained on the board for a long time, and there has never been any kind of internal dissension. There are not too many other leading clubs who can say that, with the possible exception of Arsenal. Rumours of bids and takeovers, and arguments between individual directors, may be no concern of the players, but they inevitably do affect what happens out on the pitch. Look at Manchester United and Spurs. It may sound like a cliche, but Anfield has become like a large family, with people pulling hard for each other, and that is the way to achieve good results. There have been no personality conflicts here in my time, with individuals seeking personal glory. Even great players like Keegan and Dalglish have always worked for the team, and the same can be said of the people behind the scenes. No one person has ever considered himself bigger than the club".

Tall, elegant and invariably polite, Peter Robinson's style is unmistakable. A workaholic, who thinks nothing of putting in a 12 or 15-hour day, he pays great attention to detail and leaves very little to chance. Indeed, if he has a weakness, it is that he insists on doing virtually everything himself, and finds it extremely hard to delegate, whether over the sale of tickets, the issue of information to the media, the running of the club shop, the rearrangement of fixtures, or the drawing up of player's contracts. Although he never, but never, interferes with the playing side, he is closely involved in every other aspect of the club's activities, supervising them personally to make sure there is no danger of a slip-up. Fortunately, as his health has generally been extremely good and the club operate with a small administrative staff, it has been possible for him to direct the entire operation. What would happen in the unexpected event of his illness or departure, only time will indicate.

One of Mr Robinson's major assets is his friendliness and approachability. He must have more friends than any other man in Europe, both personal and professional, with people fairly queueing up to do him and the club what favours they can. His personal contacts, allied with those of other staff members, are the envy of football and there are few players anywhere whose performances are not well known at Anfield. Moreover, the situation is much the same on the Continent. With Robinson's help, the club have excellent contacts from Iceland to Germany and from Turkey to Portugal, Ever the diplomat, he has somehow managed to avoid antagonising the most bloody-minded bureaucrats, and to ensure that Liverpool's name continues to be respected, even in Belgium in the wake of Heysel.

Within the Club, he has the invaluable asset of first class communication, seemingly able to talk to and be trusted by directors, players, ground staff, cleaners and shop assistants. All come to him for help or advice from time to time, whether over intimate personal problems or clauses in contracts involving thousands of pounds. The wonder is that he has enough time left to go home in the evening, particularly as he makes himself personally responsible for briefing the media and making sure that the daily shoal of enquiries, many of them probing deeply into confidential matters, are answered satisfactorily.

Although he is too modest to mention it, Robinson's special brand of dedication to duty has been a major factor in Liverpool's progress. Unable to play soccer seriously as a boy because of rheumatic fever, he decided to become an administrator instead, at a time when most football management was very much by rule-of-thumb. Joining little Stockport County as an office boy at 18, he soon learned the art of economy and survival the hard way, at a club where every penny counted. Still living near Northwich, he was on the bus to work by 6.30 am most mornings, frequently stayed late in the office, and devoted his evenings to studying for his chartered secretary exams. Once qualified, he won promotion as secretary to Crewe, where he virtually ran the administrative side of the club single-handed, with the help of a part-time office girl, and even took the gate money home with him, because the Crewe club could not afford a safe. Highlight of his two-year stay at Gresty Road was an F.A. Cup tie with the mighty Spurs of Blanchflower, White and Mackay, which ended in a replay after a 2-2 draw. "What with handling the sale of tickets, co-operating with the Police over crowd control and trying to help with the publicity, it was a hectic time", he recalls. "Some nights I didn't get home until the early hours. The replay was a bit of a shock too. When our train arrived in London it pulled into platform 13, and I said to someone that I hoped it wasn't an omen. Unfortunately it was, because we were beaten 13-2!"

From Crewe, Peter Robinson moved on to another unfashionable little club, Scunthorpe, where he stayed for four years, before his penultimate move to Brighton. While at Scunthorpe, he was married to his wife Dorothy, whom he had originally met when at Crewe, and again demonstrated his devotion to duty by being back at his desk in Scunthorpe first thing next morning.

123

"We had a match then, and there was nothing else I could do", he says in typically matter-of-fact way. "Football is a demanding activity, and you cannot be involved in it without making sacrifices. The first and only time I have been away from Liverpool for more than a week, in a period of more than 25 years, was when I went to watch the last World Cup competiton in Italy. And even then, I was on duty. I know it is hard on my wife and daughter (Tracy) but fortunately they have always been very understanding. Even when I have been away with Dorothy for a few days, I have always kept in touch by phone, because in this business instant availability can often make the difference when it comes to signing an outstanding player. Football is highly competitive, and nobody is going to hang around waiting for you".

His early years at Anfield drove home the message that when it comes to signing players, there is just no substitute for the best. "We had a lot of success in the early sixties, but that fine team started to grow older and we did not manage to find replacements of the calibre we needed", he points out. "Bill did sign Emlyn Hughes, who was a fine buy, but we missed out on three or four other players who might have helped us stay at the top. We offered £50,000 for Gordon Banks just before the 1966 World Cup but Leicester wouldn't part, and we also failed to sign both Mike England (who went to Spurs instead) and Peter Osgood. We even made an enquiry about Geoff Hurst, before he became a regular first teamer with West Ham, but they wanted Ron Yeats in exchange and Shanks wanted to keep him. I don't know if we tried hard enough in one or two cases, but in later years we have generally managed to get our man!

"The signing of both Kevin Keegan and Ray Clemence came about directly as a result of my connections with Scunthorpe. People were taken aback when we paid out more than £400,000 for Kenny Dalglish, because that was an enormous amount of money at the time, but it was less than we had received from Hamburg for Kevin, and I don't think anyone would say now that he was not worth the money.

"I have always been a strong supporter of the star system in professional football. Like it or not, we are in the entertainment business, and the supporters like to see new faces. In my view a club should have at least one or two exciting newcomers on view each season if it possibly can. Obviously it saves a lot of money if you can develop some of your own players, but that is always difficult at a club like Liverpool, because there is such a gulf between first team and reserves. We are so involved in winning things, that it is rarely possible to give a promising player the chance to gain experience in the first team.

"In fact, the Merseyside area has not produced many really outstanding prospects recently. Some years ago you found them with other big clubs, even if they did not end up with Liverpool or Everton, but that has not been the case for several years now. These things tend to go in cycles, so we hope it may be our turn again soon.

"Experience is so important, as it is in any professional activity. After all, you wouldn't expect a doctor or a lawyer or a businessman to stay indefinitely with the firm he starts with, would you? It's much the same in football. A player needs to move once or twice to widen his experience if he hopes to reach the top".

During his spell at Anfield, Robinson has outlasted six chairmen, five managers and a hundred or more outstanding players. "That may sound a lot of people, but really there has been considerable continuity", he emphasises. "So far as the chairmen and managers are concerned, there has usually been a clear-cut succession, with everyone simply moving up one place each time. The pattern with managers was set when Bob Paisley took over from Bill Shankly, and was succeeded in turn by Joe Fagan, though Kenny Dalgish was pitched in at the deep end while he was still playing, and Graeme Souness returned from another club.

The quiet man behind the scenes. Peter Robinson stands smiling below a banner proclaiming Liverpool's international status.

THE GLORY THAT WAS ROME

"It has probably helped that we have had so much stability among our backroom staff, so that the system of training has changed very little over more than 20 years. People have generally known what they are expected to do, and there has been plenty of experience around to provide advice when it has been required. We have also, as a matter of deliberate policy, tried to leave our managers as free as possible to concentrate on the football side of things, rather as they do on the Continent. For most of the time the club has been run by a kind of troika, with decisions being made by the chairman, the manager and myself in tandem. So far as transfers are concerned, the manager says what he wants, the chairman makes sure the money is available, and I set up the actual transfer.

"We have managed to keep most of our big deals secret, because once it leaks out that tends to prejudice bargaining. I think our best performance in that respect was when we signed Ian Rush back from Juventus. The first time anyone knew of it outside the club was when we called a conference, and Ian Rush walked into the room. Once you broadcast what you are hoping to do, you have little chance of achieving it".

Despite all the precautions, and all the help they are given, it is clearly a tremendous strain being manager of a club like Liverpool. "I don't think anyone outside football realises just what pressures a manager comes under", says Robinson. "On Merseyside more than most places, there is a continual hunger for success that is never quite satisfied. When a team win the Cup or the League, they are told 'Celebrate tonight — but be back in for training tomorrow morning". You get nothing for yesterday in this business".

Even when Liverpool won both the League Championship and the European Cup in 1977, and also reached the F.A. Cup Final, they did not rest on their laurels. Within a few days of their return from Rome, Peter Robinson was sitting down in a hotel outside Merseyside with chairman John Smith and manager Bob Paisley to outline policy for the next season. The three knew that Kevin Keegan was leaving and that one or two older players like Tommy Smith needed to be replaced, and they had no intention of being caught napping. In came Dalglish, to be followed soon after by Graeme Souness, and 12 months later Liverpool were collecting Europe's premier trophy again.

"Everyone was taken by surprise when Bill Shankly decided to call it a day, and even now there is speculation as to why he went", Robinson recalls. "He had been with us for 14 years and was thought of as a permanant fixture. You can put forward all kinds of reasons, but I honestly believe it was an accumulation of a lot of small things. In the end, the pressure became too much. Similarly, Kenny Dalglish

126

decided he could not carry on any longer for much the same reason. It is not a question of money or wanting a new challenge. It is the pressure of always striving to improve, and of knowing there are thousands of people outside expecting you to deliver the goods every time. Even finishing runners-up in the League or reaching the Cup Final is regarded as failure here. Not by the directors, but by the players themselves and their supporters. That may account for much of Liverpool's success but it is success that is only achieved at a price. To stay top, we have to work harder than everyone else, as well as play better football''.

The professional football scene has also become a lot more complicated. When Robinson first arrived at Anfield, the maximum wage had only been abolished a few years previously and players still conducted their own negotiations. Nowadays, when Peter Robinson sits down to set up a transfer, to or from Liverpool, he has to deal with a player's agent, his accountant and probably his lawyer, as well as the player himself. "You would hardly believe the complications", he says. "Few deals are straightforward, with most containing clauses regarding extra payments to be made in special circumstances, like winning a cap or playing a specific number of first team matches. There are signing-on fees to be considered, and I have even been asked for a loyalty bonus.

"Sponsorship has burst on the scene in a big way. We were the first club in England to set up a shirt advertising deal, with Hitachi, when the rules were changed to allow it. Television has become a major factor, and so have things like executive boxes. When I came here in the first place, virtually all our income came through gate receipts, but we couldn't possibly survive on gate money now, with payments to players and staff alone exceeding £5.5 million a year. Football is becoming more and more commercial all the time, and is very much a business as well as a sport. I can remember when players were paid a maximum of £20 a week, but nowadays some earn more than 200 times that amount".

So how on earth do clubs like Liverpool and Everton manage to compete with the likes of Spurs, Arsenal and Manchester United, all of whom are based in far more prosperous areas. Robinson comes right back to his first point, superior management. "Everton and ourselves remain among the cheapest clubs in the country", he points out. "It is cheaper to sit in Everton's Gwladys Street stand than it is to stand at Chelsea. We simply cannot push our prices beyond what our fans can afford, and you must realise there are thousands of people without a job on Merseyside. You can understand how tough the competition is, when I say that a full house at Anfield brings in less than half as much as a full house at Tottenham.

"Fortunately we are able to compete, because the team's success over many years has made us not just a local club but a national one and even an international one. When we carried out a survey recently, we discovered that 27 per cent of our season ticket holders came from outside Merseyside. When we play away in places like London, probably more than half our support is also from out of town. We have a Norwegian supporters club with more than 2,000 members, another large one in Germany, and we correspond regularly with a Liverpool supporters club in Poland which has its own premises. I think Manchester United are probably the only other English club who enjoy this kind of situation. I know that when we played Arsenal in Singapore, the promoters put souvenir club mugs on sale, and they sold six times as many Liverpool mugs as Arsenal ones. Similarly, our kit manufacturers tell me that the majority of our replica outfits are purchased from outside Merseyside".

Liverpool's international reputation suffered a terrible blow through the Heysel disaster of 1985. "It was absolutely dreadful. I couldn't believe it, even though I was there", says Peter Robinson. "We had played in Europe so often without the slightest hint of trouble, and suddenly I was watching Liverpool fans charging at Italians. From time to time I still wake up in the middle of the night and see bodies all round me. It was a nightmare, like finding yourself in the middle of a battlefield. You cannot forgive the people who caused it, the hooligans who rushed round wielding iron bars, but the organisers were also very much to blame. We had already protested to UEFA about the state of the ground, and the way the tickets had been sold, and they had taken no notice.

"I am afraid it will be a long time before Heysel is forgotten, because it was shown live on television all over the world. It was an international incident, and brought hundreds of reporters and camera crews flying over to Merseyside to photograph the so-called assassins. Even though we are now back in Europe after a six-year ban, the memory will live on for many years. A number of our fans were so sickened by Heysel that they have not watched us since, though some have come back. Almost the one good thing that did come out of it, was that it strengthened our ties with Juventus. We

Opposite:
"Here's to the next one." Peter Robinson and Bob Paisley toast a few of the club's trophies, including the European Cup, the Charity Shield and the Championship Cup.

were always quite close, and we have remained such good friends that they backed our return to European competition".

If Heysel was bad, Hillsborough was even worse, a disaster that so affected Peter Robinson that he came close to quitting. "To be involved in one disaster was bad enough, but two was almost unbelievable", he points out. "This time it was not foreign supporters who suffered, but our own. I suppose some abroad will have seen Hillsborough as a kind of judgement for what happened at Heysel, but all I know is that it caused an immense amount of suffering. The moment I saw that trouble was developing I went straight over to the danger area to see for myself, and when some people started to blame our supporters for breaking down the gates at Leppings Lane, I was able to demonstrate that this was not true, and show the Police that they had been opened. That disaster would have been the end of some clubs, but somehow it bound the people of Merseyside together even more closely, and I do mean Merseyside. The Everton supporters were magnificent. They stood by us in every way, even though their team had got through to Wembley the same day, and they must have been dreadfully disappointed to see that achievement rendered almost irrelevant.

"It is a very small consolation to know that Hillsborough triggered off the Taylor Report, which should result in making all big grounds considerably safer. We had no hesitation agreeing to make Anfield all-seater, because although it will cut our capacity, we cannot afford to take even the slightest risk of being involved in any sort of tragedy again. All-seater grounds are a sign of the times, and hopefully a good sign. I think that today we are looking at a new breed of supporter, who is no longer prepared to stand out in all kinds of weather, drink a cup of tea out of a plastic container and be content with a meat pie. The supporter of today and tomorrow needs a seat, good toilet facilities, enjoyable refreshments and plentiful parking space for his car".

So why has it taken so long to provide all these eminently desirable features? Robinson has no doubts. "Most English clubs play in old grounds that were built in the wrong place", he agrees. "But it isn't easy to move away from them. There is no room for large scale parking near Anfield, and we have had great difficulty even getting to a situation where we could enlarge the Kemlyn Road stand.

"When I first arrived, I canvassed the idea of a super stadium at Aintree, which could be used by both Liverpool and Everton and would provide all the necessary amenities, including parking. At that time, with European soccer still a novelty and both clubs booming, I think it would have worked, but it was clear neither set of supporters were willing to abandon their own ground. Nowadays, when the climate is more favourable, there isn't the money. To build the kind of stadium we would need, say a 60,000 all-seater ground, would cost so much that our joint income would not even cover the interest charges, let alone buy any new players. We would end up like the Mersey Tunnel, owing more money with every year".

So what does the future hold? Must it be all gloom and doom, or is there a brave new future? And will Merseyside's two giants continue to play a leading part? Characteristically, Mr Robinson is both positive and optimistic. One of the first to envisage the kind of super league that the F.A. have proposed. He is sure that an independent Premier Division will not only provide better entertainment for its members, but can help to revive the fortunes of the smaller clubs as well.

"The Football League had become unmanageable in its present form. It is as simple as that", he emphasises. "The needs of the big First Division clubs are totally different from those of the remainder. We need to have the freedom to employ professional marketing experts, men who can tie up big television deals, high calibre sponsorships, and really sell the best football to the public. Obviously there must continue to be promotion and relegation, because no sporting body can exist in a vacuum, and ambitious clubs must have a target they know is attainable. But that doesn't mean the clubs in divisions two, three and four cannot carry out their own deals or run their own competitions. If they set about it properly there is no reason why they shouldn't be better off than before.

"So far as Europe is concerned, I think we are seeing the start of something significant with the last stages of the European Cup being played off in two divisions like the World cup. I suspect that will extend to the other two European events, and that it will be very popular. I don't think people really want more European competition than that. If it becomes too frequent, it will lose much of its appeal, because whereas it has a certain novelty at the moment, I doubt if the British public want to watch Continental-style games every week".

Can Merseyside retain its pre-eminent position, at least in England? I don't see why not. Both our clubs have an excellent manager and some very good players, and both have a lot of experience. One of the best features of recent years is that although we continue to be great rivals, we have a lot of respect for each other. In fact there have been two or three recent transfers to Goodison from Anfield which appear to have been quite successful. Merseyside fans have shown that it is possible to keep great rivalry within sporting limits, and I think the finals we have contested at Wembley have been enjoyed throughout the country. Just as Merseysiders came through the Blitz more determined than ever, so I think our clubs will emerge from the tragedies and trials of recent years ready to challenge successfully for the highest domestic and European honours. One thing is certain, the passion is still there. We can fill Anfield every Saturday and even the advent of seats will not diminish the fans' enthusiasm. The Kop still chant Bill Shankly's name, though many of the younger supporters were not even born when he was in charge".

Archbishop Derek Worlock

Unlike most of the other leading characters in this book, Archbishop Derek Worlock does not consider himself a Liverpudlian. Unashamedly a Man of Hampshire, he neither found himself in the city through birth, nor volunteered to go there. Instead he was sent, some will say through divine inspiration, to do a specific job for the Roman Catholic Church, and one that he has done magnificently. Indeed, his contribution has rather been to the whole of the Christian movement, rather than just a part of it, for together with his Anglican counterpart Bishop David Sheppard he has led such a crusade against sectarianism and intolerance that it has become widely known as the Mersey Miracle.

So strong have become the links between Roman Catholic and Anglican communities, reinforced more recently by similar links with the Free Churches, that for once Christianity has been able to speak with a single voice. And as Merseyside has struggled to overcome urban deprivation, social injustice, a chronic shortage of investment, the notorious Toxteth riots and two terrible football disasters, that voice of informed, sympathetic reason has become ever more relevant. Whatever else may be wrong with Liverpool and its surrounding districts today, its churches are setting a proud example to the rest of the country.

Born in a flat overlooking Lord's cricket ground (an interesting coincidence in view of Rev. David Sheppard's Test connections) to parents who were converted to the Roman Catholic faith during a seven-year engagement, Derek Worlock says he cannot remember a time when he did not wish to become a priest. This was probably due in at least some part to family tradition, as no fewer than 12 of his ancestors had taken Holy Orders, including one who was involved in the battle of Dettingen as a military chaplain way back in 1743.

At his first school, a preparatory at Winchester, he soon learned what it was like to be a man alone. "In recognition of freedom of conscience I was not required to attend the school chapel or morning chapel in the school library", he recalls in the book "Better Together" that he wrote in partnership with Bishop Sheppard. "I spent many a lonely hour in the corridor outside, increasingly doubting the nature of my privilege. But I recall the hurt from the taunts of other boys that I was a 'foreigner' or untouchable. In those days there were even fewer sensitivities among small boys than there are today".

The constant sense of persecution strengthened rather than weakened Derek Worlock's resolve, partly due to a strong sense of tradition because, as he says: "The need to resist any requirement to conform was an important element in the faith of English Catholics, and part of our inherited pride in the sacrifices of martyrs in previous centuries". When a fellow pupil insulted the Pope, they came to blows, and the future Archbishop suffered the indignity of a caning in consequence.

Even after he left prep. school, progress into the Church was barred by opposition from his local Bishop, who felt he came from the wrong background, and it was only after a certain amount of subterfuge that he was accepted into St. Edmund's College at Ware in 1934. There, he experienced further separatism, because the college was divided into three houses, two for pupils and one for those hoping to enter the Ministry.

"We learned from our fellow students the value of community, but we were taught to be self-sufficient and adaptable", he recalls. "The six-year withdrawal from the world constituted in itself a formidable test. In my case most of it coincided with the Second World War, and this made it more difficult to sustain. As theological students, we were classified as having reserved occupations, and not subject to call-up. Not many of us were given the 'white feather' treatment, but when relatives and friends were killed, the pressure to at least postpone one's training was acute. In this most difficult situation I was most encouraged by my brother, who soon afterwards was lost at sea".

Derek Worlock did not miss the ravages of war entirely. Ordained in Westminster Cathedral a few days before D-Day, he was appointed curate to a parish in that diocese and arrived there just as the flying bomb onslaught began. "I administered the sacrament of annointing over 50 times before I had a case of natural death", he recalls. Later, a flying bomb landed almost on top of the presbytery, killing nearly 50 people, and destroying the church. Had he not flung himself to the ground in the nick of time he too would have been among the victims.

His training over, Derek Worlock was appointed secretary to the Archbishop of Westminster, Cardinal Bernard Griffin, a post he was to hold under three different incumbents. And quite apart from the

Opposite:
The true spirit of ecumenical understanding. Archbishop Derek Worlock with his close friend and Christian partner, the Rev. David Sheppard.

135

invaluable experience his new role gave him in the fields of communication and public relations, it also left him in no doubt about the yawning gap which then existed between the Anglican and Roman Catholic Churches. The famous joint letters to the Times, during the war, which had emphasised the unity of all the Churches in a common cause, had been discontinued because of a row over precedence, and the atmosphere grew ever more frigid. "There was almost no collaboration, for example, regarding the immense amount of post-war legislation", says Derek Worlock. "Nor was help sought or given as religious persecution grew in Eastern Europe. These difficulties and differences arose mainly from the failure to recognise what we would now regard as essential Christian bonds".

Whatever his personal feelings may have been, Derek Worlock would not have been able to achieve any of the great successes of his later career, had there not been a dramatic change of heart at the top. But in October 1958, Angelo Roncalli was elected to the Papacy as Pope John 13, and immediately announced his intention to call an ecumenical council at the Vatican. There followed his famous encyclical letter on "Truth, Unity and Peace" which contained the significant and inspiring phrase "Unity in essentials, freedom in uncertainties, in all things charity". At long last, the way to a closer understanding between the churches and their people had been opened.

The Second Vatican Council, which eventually opened in October 1962, was to prove one of the great formative events of Derek Worlock's life. He served as secretary to the English-speaking bishops, was appointed an expert consultant on the role of the laity, and served as a member of the sub-committee charged with writing documents of family life and the socio-economic order, which had gradually become his specialist interest. Probably even more significantly, as it was to turn out, he met and became friendly with the Polish Archbishop who was to become Pope John Paul 2.

Ecumenical change, of course, took time to evolve and it was not long before Derek Worlock had forsaken the high academic debate of the Vatican for the much more down to earth environment of London's East End. After serving three Archbishops as secretary he was allowed to return to parish priesthood, and enjoyed what he says were the happiest 18 months of his life as Dean and Parish Priest of

Opposite:
A moment to cherish. Archbishop Worlock greets Pope Paul during the latter's visit to Liverpool.

136

St. Mary and St. Michael's in Stepney. "The care of Souls for the first time, the warm parish family life, the cheerful solidarity of East End Dockers, a vast church which on occasion we could fill, a new presbytery and schools to replace those destroyed in the war, and best of all five priests of my own choice, I was indeed a happy man", he says.

Much of his experience in the East End was to prove of special value later in Liverpool, and he also made a couple of significant contacts. One was the formidable Rector of Stepney, Rev. Edwyn Young, with whom Worlock became friendly and whom he was to meet again in Liverpool; the other was a youthful David Sheppard. "I regret to say that I can remember no more than an expressed willingness to meet again once I had settled in", he recalls. "I never dreamed he would become so friendly or that we would achieve so much together".

That short period of bliss in Stepney was followed by a period of just over 10 years as Bishop of Portsmouth, in his home county of Hampshire. That was also an enjoyable time, in a pleasant part of the country far removed from either the East End or Liverpool, but the new Bishop was acquiring experience with every month and doing his best to encourage ecumenism, not an easy task when only one in 20 of Hampshire's population at the time was a Catholic. Even so, it must have been a considerable culture shock as well as an immense challenge, when he was suddenly told, in February 1976, that the Pope had chosen him to succeed the ailing Archbishop of Liverpool, George Andrew Beck. On Sunday, March 14 he travelled to Liverpool by train to take up his new appointment. "The front doorbell rang, and one of the few faces I knew came round the door. Armed with a bottle of wine, my first visitor, Bishop David Sheppard (who had himself been appointed less than a year previously) had come to say 'Welcome'". It was the most appropriate way to start a partnership that was to have such significant results for the city of Liverpool.

In view of what was to happen later, many people have expressed surprise at the supposed coincidence that placed these two religious leaders in the same city at the same time. However it is now crystal clear that it was no accident, and that the hierarchy of both churches thought long and hard before they selected men whom they felt would be able to work together. "When the question of replacing my predecessor arose, the diocese specifically asked for someone prepared to encourage change, not only with regard to inter-Church relations, but the change needed to help combat social conditions that had been steadily worsening, Archbishop Worlock told me: "The Pope and others were aware of my experience in Stepney, and they believed I would be able to co-operate with Bishop Sheppard, without either of us having to compromise his basic beliefs. They were right".

"Our personal friendship may be a bonus, but it is very real. We respect each other greatly, based on the acceptance of each other's baptism. The key factor, is that we share responsibility for the spread of the Gospel. We have come to work together so regularly, that there is rarely a day when Bishop David and I do not talk to each other on the 'phone if not in person, rarely a week when we are not involved in some project together, rarely a month when we are not paying a joint visit.

"Liverpool prescribed a particular problem, because of its sectarian history. It is a fact that Cardinal Heenan was once stoned by Protestants when he visited members of his diocese in a so-called Orange district, but I am confident that could not happen today. From the moment I arrived in Liverpool, I was determined that hatred and distrust of that kind should be broken down, and that the city should never become another Belfast. And talking of Belfast, Bishop David and I have paid several joint visits to that city. Both of us have refused to go alone, because we felt our presence together was essential to get over the essential message of Christian unity. We would not claim to have achieved anything substantial over there, but we believe we have learned a great deal and our example may just have helped. We don't go there with solutions, but we do try to share their burden.

"Of course you have to work at a partnership like this if it has to have any real meaning. That takes time, but it is a great pleasure. Whenever we can, we make joint statements on major social issues, but if either of us is away for any reason, the other knows he can safely speak for both. We even keep a large double diary for our joint engagements, and a double record book to list all that has occurred. It is hard work but immensely worthwhile, and essential if those who would like to open the old divisions are to be prevented from doing so".

From the very first Good Friday after his arrival, Derek Worlock and David Sheppard have made a point of meeting on that day 'at the foot of the Cross' to discuss their faith, privately but openly, and eight years later they jointly presented a large wooden crucifix to the first Anglican/Catholic church built by their two dioceses. The pair have attended services in each other's cathedrals, something that would have been unthinkable not so long ago, and repeatedly helped each other with joint projects.

History in the making. Archbishop Worlock accompanies Bishop David Sheppard and Free Church Moderator Dr. John Newton down the aptly-named Hope Street to demonstrate Church unity.

Other churches, notably the Methodist, the Salvation Army and the United Reformed have also come to be involved in the Merseyside drive for unity. By happy coincidence the thoroughfare linking the Anglican and Metropolitan Cathedrals is called Hope Street, and in recent years there have been a number of symbolic marches down it by members of the various church congregations. The first took place in Jubilee Year (1977) when members celebrated the Jubilee in their own churches on the Sunday morning, and then united in a service of thanksgiving and celebration starting in the Anglican Cathedral and continuing in its neighbour. Later, Hope Street was jammed for the visit of the Pope in 1982, which saw him pray with 'The other Churches' in the Anglican Cathedral before celebrating Mass in his own.

By 1985 ecumenism had progressed so far that a great Covenanting service was held in the two Cathedrals. "There was a huge congregation for the opening of the Service in the Metropolitan Cathedral, where Dean Patey, who had returned to Liverpool from retirement, preached of the sign which this historic step might be to the nation", says Derek Worlock. "Then we moved in procession to the Anglican Cathedral, gathering numbers on the way. When we looked back it was to see Hope Street filled with a joyful surge of people from all parts of Merseyside and of all ages. Afterwards we were told 'If the Church leaders had wanted to turn back they could not. The crowd would have carried them forward".

So influential has the Merseyside ecumenical movement become, that Liverpool was chosen for the launch of a major national crusade in September 1990, when thousands of Christians visited the city to see the inauguration of a brand new organisation, the Council of Churches for Britain and Ireland. Apart from Archbishop Worlock, Bishop Sheppard and Dr. John Newton, moderator of the Free Churches on Merseyside, those attending included the Archbishop of Canterbury (Dr. Robert Runcie), Cardinal Basil Hume, Archbishop of Westminster and the Most Rev. John Hapgood, Archbishop of York. Said Dr. Newton: "The new Council is the most representative body of Christians to exist since the Reformation. It is a tremendous step forward, and can produce spin-offs for the entire community".

Such spin-offs are undoubted. The growing unity between the various churches and their leaders, has undoubtedly helped them exert much greater influence on the conduct of life in Liverpool, and become involved in major social topics like housing, unemployment and racialism.

Racialism has been a particularly sore topic in Liverpool, with many whites denying it even exists, and the coloureds claiming they suffer severely from discrimination. "When I arrived in Liverpool I found only small numbers of black people in church", says Archbishop Worlock. "We met little or none of the black-led churches, so strong in settled black communities. Liverpool has had a substantial black community for at least 100 years. Yet we found there were no Black M.P.s or city councillors, and hardly any Liverpool-born lawyers, doctors, teachers, managers or, for that matter, clergy. We met a whole community which felt itself excluded from the normal workings and opportunity of the city which was their home".

It was the disadvantagement of the coloured community that is generally thought to have been behind the notorious Toxteth riots, one of the worst scars on Liverpool's post-war history. Archbishop

Worlock felt the problems keenly, and did all he could to prevent the trouble escalating. "I spent the whole night down there, trying to prevent the Police going in", he recalls. "In the end I managed to smuggle in a microphone for the use of Wally Brown, one of the community leaders, and he persuaded most of the rioters to go home. It was a very complicated issue, and although none can excuse the damage done, many of the people there had very genuine grievances. The important thing we tried to emphasise was reconciliation.

"I used that word myself when I was interviewed on Brian Redhead's programme, and it was vital if we were to avoid a repetition of that terrible situation. The black leaders approached us for help, and so did the Chief Constable, Ken Oxford. The two sides could not meet directly and asked us to sit in the middle. Our role had to be that of sensitive communicators, trying to make each other aware of the other's hopes and needs and fears. It was not just a question of being honest brokers, they had to feel they could trust us completely. In fact it was what I would call intelligent communication, and I am thankful to say that it worked. No-one could pretend we solved all the problems, but I think there has at least been a growing awareness of what they are, and a much bigger effort by all parties to solve them".

Archbishop and Bishop have frequently tried to intervene to ease the pain caused by factory closures, but all too often their efforts have been in vain. "To try and create an awareness of the extent of what was happening, we convened a number of weekend conferences under the title: 'Work-or-What?' says Derek Worlock. "It was abundantly clear that unemployment on Merseyside was not cyclical but chronic". Initially, he encountered nothing but suspicion from both sides, even trade union members openly asking what clergymen knew about industrial relations. But after the Archbishop had joined a march to protest against the closure of the Dunlop factory, in company with Bishop Sheppard and the Methodist chairman, Norman Denny, it gradually came to be accepted that the churches were not only willing to help, but could occasionally exert valuable influence.

"People came to realise that we were sometimes able to open doors, at least for consultation", says Derek Worlock. "They did not expect us to support them — right or wrong. During the 'Winter of

Opposite:
Church and State. Archbishop Worlock greets former Prime Minister Margaret Thatcher to point out some of the City's economic problems.

142

Discontent' we received many requests for guidance. And that was before the entire industrial situation changed with the election of Mrs Thatcher's Government. People sometimes accused us of becoming involved in political matters that were not our business. I can only reply that those who claim to follow Jesus Christ must, like him, work for the interests of the poor and deprived".

One of the advantages of increased involvement, has been the development of important contacts. "A young businessman came to see me once, and asked if I could help him contact a particular Government department", says Archbishop Worlock. "He had been trying for some time, but been passed on from one person to another. Fortunately, I knew someone in a senior position there, from past dealings with the Department, and I was able to make a few telephone calls and put the businessman in touch with the right person. The order concerned was worth several million pounds, so it was obviously helpful to the area.

"I am afraid that in many ways, it still remains a tale of two cities. The centre is fine, with many exciting new developments; other areas are terribly deprived, with a great many people out of work, living in poor conditions and having little hope for the future. The philosophy of the Government appears to have been that if companies are enabled to make substantial profits, some of the benefits will gradually trickle down to the people at the bottom. That simply doesn't happen, and I find such a policy socially unacceptable.

"There seems to be less money available for things like hospitals and the social services, and more and more dependence on what I would call credit card charity. It is comforting that people remain willing to put their hands in their pockets to help others, but in my view that should never be expected to take the place of social responsibility by and for the entire community.

"Liverpool is not alone, but it has certainly suffered serious deprivation in recent years. It has had a very bad image outside, despite the efforts of people like Jim Fitzpatrick of the Dock Board, who used to remind everyone that even if Liverpool dockers were often the first out, they were also the first back. That has also made Liverpudlians rather inward-looking. It goes back to the old family spirit, which made all the members stand together, and which was carried on by the influx of Irish immigrants of the last century. They found they had to stick together to survive, and although there are not many migrants from Ireland here now, the same attitude continues".

For all his involvement with Liverpool's cause, Derek Worlock remains a Hampshire man at heart. His first visit to Anfield came when Southampton were playing there, and he recalls being the only person sitting silent in the directors' box when Liverpool scored. However, his commitment has now become total, and he tells me that he has no plans to move elsewhere. "Those terrible disasters of Heysel and Hillsborough brought us all close together", he points out. "After Heysel, the Church leaders joined in a communal service at Anfield, which I think was appreciated, and we were all heavily involved after Hillsborough. That was an occasion when the good natural qualities in almost everyone emerged. I think that for once, even those living a long way away from Merseyside were able to appreciate the special nature of its people.

"We all came together to help each other and give strength to the bereaved, in what was a magnificent show of solidarity. That word emerged in connection with Poland in 1980, and I fear it is often misunderstood. It is sometimes thought of as militancy, but militancy is really only a part of solidarity, which is a tremendous communal quality, and basically unselfish. The solidarity of Merseyside people is probably the area's greatest asset, and one I much admire".

Unity, co-operation and solidarity. These are among the main legacies that Archbishop Worlock will ultimately leave to his adopted city, a place he has done so much to help. Together with his great friend and collaborator, David Sheppard, he has laboured long and hard to bring comfort where there was once sadness, and hope where there was once very little. In an increasingly materialistic age, where so much is measured by honours or money, their example has been invaluable. Perhaps others outside Merseyside would do well to heed it.